ALL RISE

ALL RISE

PRACTICAL TOOLS FOR BUILDING HIGH-PERFORMANCE LEGAL TEAMS

BENJAMIN SACHS

LIONCREST
PUBLISHING

ALL RISE
Practical Tools for Building High-Performance Legal Teams

ISBN   978-1-5445-3724-5   *Hardcover*
       978-1-5445-3725-2   *Paperback*
       978-1-5445-3726-9   *Ebook*

To EMS, RJS, & OHS, my all-time favorite team.

CONTENTS

INTRODUCTION

"I had to leave my law firm to learn about great management."

This was a colleague I had known for more than a decade, one who had spent many years at a top global firm before moving on to a series of in-house executive roles in technology companies. He had just started a new general counsel role, and we were discussing the challenge of building great legal teams.

"In other industries, especially tech, they recognize management as a *science*," he explained. "Knowing what I know now, if I went back to Big Law today, I would run my teams completely differently."

I shared his sentiment. After starting my career at a large firm, I took a detour to work at Boston Consulting Group, a strategic management consulting firm, where I set aside my legal skills for two years to learn the language of business. I expected BCG to teach me about strategy, financial structures, corporate transformations, and more, which I thought would ultimately make me a better lawyer. That was all true, but it turned out that the most valuable lessons BCG taught me had nothing to do with the mechanics of big business.

Even though consulting and law firms have aspects in common—a global footprint, large corporate clients, intense hours, and hierarchies governed by partners—they had entirely different approaches to building teams. At BCG, teaming was considered its own *discipline*. Leaders shared best practices and advice to sharpen their management skills. Junior team members were encouraged to give feedback to team leaders and partners freely, and they routinely did so, not behind the cover of anonymous surveys, but face-to-face.

Fast forward many years to when I was General Counsel and Chief Operating Officer at a technology company, overseeing not just legal work but teams of analysts, engineers, marketers, product managers, designers, and more. Developing management principles that worked across law and business forced me to be more intentional about every aspect of leadership, and I was surrounded by equally committed colleagues ready with ideas and feedback so we could improve together. We were as analytical about how we ran our teams as we were about the products we developed.

By contrast, many law firms and other legal organizations do not adopt a rigorous approach to how they build and support teams. One senior partner at a large firm told me, "Partners here are a bit like feudal lords. We report to someone, of course, just like feudal lords all served the king. But as long as we pay our proper tribute, we are largely left to govern our people as we see fit."

This freedom can be a curse. Without a common approach to building strong teams, each office or each practice group of a large organization can feel like a distinct entity, with its own idiosyncratic rules and styles for how work gets done. Not only does this result in wildly inconsistent approaches, but it is terribly inefficient, leaving many attorneys to reinvent the wheel. Some will develop into wonderful managers, but they tend to be the exception, rather than the norm.

NOT WHETHER, BUT WHY

These challenges are well-known in our industry. In teaching and consulting for attorneys, I hear complaints about systemic dysfunction and poor management in every sector, including firms, corporations, government agencies, and nonprofits. The question is not *whether* we have work to do, but *why* we have not solved the problem by now. In other industries, there are plenty of success stories. Why have so many legal organizations, especially law firms, been unable to turn the corner?

Some attorneys believe that their leaders do not take "management" seriously. But such short-sighted thinking is not as common as people might think. Nearly every law firm executive, general counsel, and legal director I meet acknowledges the gap. "If I could fix any single problem with a snap of my fingers," one government agency's division director told me, "it would be to transform our management culture."

Sadly, there are no quick fixes for what ails us. In fact, the search for quick fixes is part of the problem. Building strong teams requires attention and commitment from everyone in the organization, from the most junior attorneys to the most senior leaders. The task is so daunting that most do not even know where to start, which leads them to retreat back into legal work.

The work of building strong teams is not a billable activity one can clock in and out of like any other legal matter. No single management seminar is going to transform an attorney, a legal team, or an organization. Yet even when leaders acknowledge this limitation—when they recognize that more work is needed—they nevertheless continue to struggle with execution. We need a more systematic approach.

EXECUTION FROM TOP TO BOTTOM

If we want results, we have to rethink our execution at every level: the organization, the team, and the individual.

At the organizational level, leaders need a common framework that defines the key traits of high-performance teams. This is more than just a semantic exercise; it is about alignment. Without a common language and clear expectations for what makes a great team, everyone spirals off in a different direction, and senior leaders have no way to measure progress across all of these inconsistent approaches. The framework in this book has been battle-tested across industries for many years and is well-suited to legal organizations. (Note that the term "legal organizations" encompasses not only law firms but also nonprofit legal groups, agencies with legal divisions, and in-house legal teams of corporations.)

Precise execution is also needed at the team level. Every team is different, with its own unique subculture, pain points, and processes. The M&A practice will have different needs than Commercial Litigation, so a generic "management training" is not going to provide the kind of rich, tactical guidance each group needs to be successful. A team-centric approach means putting the entire team—such as all the associates and partners from a single practice group or regional office—in the same room to discuss their challenges and align on action items *together*. They are not merely discussing ideas; they are committing to a plan of attack. It also ensures that the discussion zeroes in on topics that truly matter. This cannot happen in a management seminar packed solely with fifth-year associates.

Finally, each individual has a role to play in helping build stronger teams. This book is not just for managers. I remember a partner at BCG sitting me down on my first day with a new case team and saying, "I expect you to make the entire team better. Just doing your work well isn't going to be good enough." I had just started my *second year*; I had never conceived of my role as anything beyond my specific silo of assignments. He took an ax to that narrow-minded attitude and forced me—and everyone on the team—to take on a shared responsibility for the team as a whole.

He was right, and the lessons apply to any profession, including law. As this book will explain, even the most junior team members can learn how to spot and diagnose problems on their team and do their part to correct them. Your leadership and influence can extend far beyond your title.

Thoughtful execution at each of these three levels—the organization, the team, and the individual—generates a powerful combined effect. But having three levels of execution also increases the risk of misalignment. That is why it is so important to adopt a unified framework for the principles that will guide us throughout this journey.

THE FRAMEWORK

Simply stated, our mission is to *build high-performance legal teams*. To do that, we have to start by defining what makes these teams special.

Regardless of the industry, high-performance teams have four key traits in common:

1. Trust: They are comfortable being honest and vulnerable
2. Ownership: They put the team's goals above personal goals
3. Productive Conflict: They challenge each other's ideas
4. Accountability: They hold each other to high standards

Trust is first for a reason. When teams falter, many team leaders focus on the failures they see in accountability, conflict avoidance, or lack of ownership. But smart leaders know that trust is often the key to turning everything around.

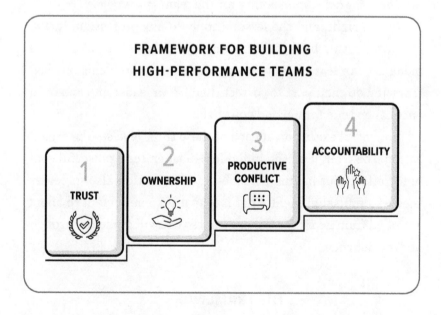

FRAMEWORK FOR BUILDING HIGH-PERFORMANCE TEAMS

1 TRUST

2 OWNERSHIP

3 PRODUCTIVE CONFLICT

4 ACCOUNTABILITY

When team members lack trust, they focus only on self-preservation. Once teams establish trust, they begin to look beyond their personal interests and focus instead on what's best for the team—the first step toward true ownership. When they feel genuine ownership over the goals of the team or organization, they readily challenge and sharpen each other's ideas, harnessing the power of productive conflict. And finally, once teams are willing to engage in conflict, they can hold each other accountable, not through a culture of fear or micromanagement, but through a common set of standards that empower *everyone* to lead.

Without these traits, a manager must pull all the strings and coach each team member through every task. But if and when teams climb this ladder to the top, everything changes. Instead of a single manager pulling team members over the finish line, team members push *each other*. They support and coach each other. They expect great things from each other, and they don't want to let their colleagues down. In this environment, the improvement is not linear; it is *exponential*. If you have ever served on such a team, you know what that difference feels like. It is a team you never want to leave.

This book will unpack the four traits of high-performance teams one by one, starting with trust. Each section will include relevant psychological and behavioral models of organizational behavior, but we are focused on turning academic into actionable. No trust falls or vague buzzwords—just sound tools that attorneys need to drive change on their teams.

TAILORED FOR ATTORNEYS

These four key traits of high-performance teams are not specific to legal teams. In fact, one of the very first books that I read on managing teams, Patrick Lencioni's *Five Dysfunctions of a Team*, continues to inspire my teaching today, despite it not being written for the legal profession, and countless other books provide general frameworks and tools that could be useful to attorneys.[1]

But despite the existence of these concepts in other industries, leadership advice often falls flat with lawyers because it fails to take into account the unique experiences and obstacles we face. This is particularly true at law firms, where cookie-cutter management tactics simply do not translate well to intense litigation and deal teams.

Some law firm partners also make the mistake of believing that investing in a stronger team culture will blunt their competitive edge. When they hear the word "culture," they bristle, thinking not of the famous quote by Peter Drucker ("Culture eats strategy for breakfast") but rather of frivolities like ping-pong tables and free snacks. But a strong culture does not require taking one's foot off the gas. I have worked with practice groups hellbent on becoming the dominant player in their markets, with leaders at the helm who understand the extraordinary work and sacrifice it will take to win. The recommendations in this book are fully compatible with those goals. In fact, they are more than compatible; they are *vital*, because ensuring peak performance is the only way such leaders will be able to reach their goals without destroying their teams (and the value they have created) in the process.

For these reasons, despite the fact that this book will offer guidance to attorneys everywhere, most of the examples will focus on attorneys in high-pressure environments where the problems are most severe. I have spent many years teaching law students and lawyers at every level of their careers, watching as many of them join large firms with a sense of eagerness, only to leave jaded. This dissatisfaction should not be their destiny.

My hope is that if we can do it in law firms, we can do it anywhere attorneys work, be it at a government agency, a legal nonprofit, or an in-house legal team. Every environment will present its own challenges; for example, agencies and nonprofits have unique constraints and stakeholder considerations that require special attention. But the tools of high-performance teams will still apply.

A note on terminology. Although most of this book will offer advice that applies to attorneys at all levels, there will be times when I want to specifically tailor the guidance to certain audiences. When I refer to "senior" attorneys or "managers," for example, that is intended to include attorneys who oversee the work of others. By contrast, I will generally refer to the people they oversee as "junior" team members. These terms have less to do with age or tenure and more to do with *context*. For example, a second-year associate can be a manager over a workstream but still feel like the junior player in a strategy meeting with partners. And even partners can feel like junior team members when they collaborate with more senior leaders.

Finally, all attorneys should keep in mind that legal teams encompass more than just lawyers. Success requires close collaboration with paralegals, assistants, IT professionals, investigators, HR experts, professional development managers, and countless others. Because writing out this list is cumbersome, I may refer to "team members" and "attorneys" interchangeably, but do not misinterpret this shorthand to suggest that the only team members that matter are those with law degrees.

THE PAYOFF

Although the challenge ahead may seem daunting, it also presents a tremendous opportunity, both for individual attorneys and for organizations as a whole. For attorneys to stand out, they

XVIII · ALL RISE

need to know not just how to spin a precedent or weave together complex deal terms. They have to know how to build and leverage incredible teams. That skill, even more than brilliant legal thinking, is what catapults careers.

It is also the key to winning the talent wars.

During the COVID-19 pandemic, the legal talent wars reached a new height. Even before the pandemic, law firms were concerned about retaining top talent. But by the end of 2021, roughly 23%—nearly *one quarter*—of associates at law firms had left their firms.[2]

At first, many thought this was just attorneys' version of the so-called Great Resignation, the pandemic-era phenomenon where many employees reexamined their career choices and chose a different path. "I had imagined associates resigning en masse to do some kind of 'Eat-Pray-Love' thing," wrote Vivia Chen, a columnist for Bloomberg Law.[3] But that was not the case. In fact, many attorneys were not leaving Big Law altogether; they were just shuffling between firms. Big Law as a whole held onto 18% *more* attorneys in 2021 than it did in 2019.[4]

At Georgetown Law, the Center on Ethics and the Legal Profession teamed up with the Thomson Reuters Institute to analyze the differences between the winners (firms with low turnover rates) and losers (firms with high turnover rates) in this great contest. You might think that firms with lower turnover paid their associates more or perhaps demanded fewer hours from them. *Neither was true.* Associates at low turnover firms worked 51 *more* hours per year and earned 16% *smaller* raises over the same period than associates at high-turnover firms.[5] Yet those firms enjoyed *half* as much turnover.

Loyalty comes from "less tangible factors," wrote the study's authors. Or, to put it more plainly: people don't quit their jobs, they quit their bosses. When attorneys feel every firm is largely the same, even a small bump in compensation (or other perks) might be enough motivation to break them away. On the other hand, when firms distinguish themselves through *how* they work—their culture, management style, professional development, and values—attorneys connect more deeply, more genuinely to the firm and to each other. These "intangibles" generate connections that are much harder to break.

But retention is just the tip of the iceberg. Stronger teams are not just happier; they *perform* better. They are more efficient and productive. They handle setbacks more smoothly. They sharpen each other's ideas through honest feedback. And they are more self-sufficient, overcoming obstacles on their own rather than seeking help from "the boss" at every turn.

Who wouldn't want these qualities on their team, whether at a legal nonprofit, a government agency, or a firm? No legal team has infinite budget, and certainly not infinite time. For senior leaders, the math is obvious. Teams that perform better and stick around longer will in turn generate better work (and more revenue), all while reducing the time and money wasted recruiting and training replacements for those who leave for greener pastures. From a P&L standpoint, it's a no-brainer.

But for individual attorneys, including the most junior associates, this is much more than a financial exercise. This is about your career—your life. So much of your life is spent at work, after all. Long nights and weekends will not evaporate completely, but strong teams have more control over their time because they are more disciplined and organized in how they approach complex assignments. They communicate better, collaborate better, and produce better work because the entire team is engaged. When you work on a team operating at this higher level, it is not an experience you ever forget.

LOOKING FORWARD

Admittedly, these were not the skills we learned in law school. This is an entirely new curriculum to most attorneys, but the chapters that follow provide a step-by-step playbook for creating high-performance legal teams. It's not magic; it's a methodical way of thinking about what drives better retention, higher leverage, and better job satisfaction using practices that have been refined in other industries yet remain elusive in the legal profession. You will gain new insights for managing "up" and "down." You will learn how to support and enhance the power of diverse teams. And you'll build more self-awareness so that you can continuously improve throughout your career.

By the end, you will see your team—its people, its strengths, and its weaknesses—in a whole new light. This is not just the path for personal growth as an attorney; it is the means for elevating your entire team. As you rise, all rise.

PART 1

TRUST

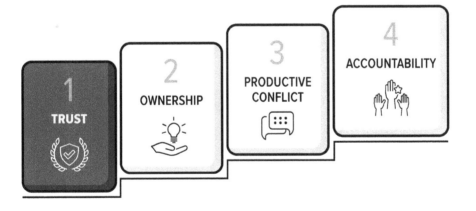

PSYCHOLOGICAL SAFETY

n 2012, Google set out to determine, with mathematical precision, the formula for the perfect team. At the time, the tech giant had more than $50B in revenue and more than 50,000 employees worldwide. Keeping this juggernaut on its upward trajectory meant constantly expanding its massive employee base, and when a company operates at that level of scale, even small improvements can make a substantial difference to its bottom line.

With that in mind, and being a pioneer in data analytics, Google turned its talents inward, conducting a study of 180 of its own teams. They examined a wide spectrum of data points to determine the factors that best predicted which teams would be successful over time. Decades of prior research (not to mention most people's intuitions) suggested that factors like education, standardized test scores, GPAs, socialization outside the office, and personality styles might play a strong part in predicting a team's success. Google being Google, they appointed data-driven experts in their People Analytics Division—yes, they have a People Analytics Division—to collect these metrics and progressively track teams' performance.

But no matter how they examined the data, they could not find any support for the notion that a specific combination of individuals with certain traits was likely to be more successful than any other. In fact, as Abeer Dubey, the head of this initiative, told the *New York Times Magazine* when the results were publicly released in 2016, "The 'who' part of the equation didn't seem to matter."[6]

Instead, one factor stood out more than any other: whether the team members had enough *trust* to take risks and be vulnerable in front of each other without fear of being embarrassed, punished, or rejected—otherwise known as "psychological safety." Teams with psychological safety achieved their goals more often and drove more value for the business. Those without it fell behind.

This study—known as Project Aristotle—was a turning point in a long debate about what makes great teams. Leadership books for many years touted the benefits of trust and psychological safety. But many leaders and executives still held on to more traditional views and sought to avoid concepts they saw as "touchy-feely" or "squishy." Now Google, a tech company with an aggressive work culture (in spite of what you may have heard about office playgrounds and catered lunches) was not only bringing mathematical proof for its assertions about what makes great teams, but they were turning these insights into actions around the company, from how they interviewed candidates, to the content of their internal trainings, to their employee assessments.

Almost overnight, every tech company was trying to follow Google's lead, and other industries were not far behind.

But there was a problem. The theories were well and good, but putting those ideas into practice became, for some, a seemingly insurmountable challenge. Every industry, not to mention every organization, is different. As the ripple effects from Project Aristotle spread to other sectors, the examples and best practices shared by Google seemed less and less applicable. Ideas are not enough, after all; the hard part is *execution*.

Law firms have been particularly slow to adapt. As lawyers, we work differently than most employees at Google. True, both environments are competitive. Both have long hours. But ours are billable. Our time is sold to clients. As lawyers, we *are* the product we sell. And while law firms work hard to tout differentiation, many clients see firms as more or less fungible, forcing us to be even more aggressive to win (and hold onto) their business. So who has time for trust-building?

The fact is, law firms and other legal organizations no longer have a choice. If we fail to build legal teams around a strong foundation of psychological safety, the lack of trust will translate directly into attrition and erode our practice groups and our business. Your associates may not use the words "trust" and "psychological safety" on the way out the door. They will talk about feeling like a cog in a machine, or not having opportunities for mentorship, or not feeling connected to the firm. But all these roads lead back to trust.

If you accept that this investment is necessary, then the question becomes: how do you put these principles into practice most efficiently? We need to turn the "soft stuff" into something more concrete. First, we have to clarify what we mean by "psychological safety."

WHAT IS PSYCHOLOGICAL SAFETY?

At its core, psychological safety is a measure of professional trust within the team: trust that team members can admit mistakes, express their honest opinions, and ask questions, all without fear of judgment or reprisal.

It may be easier to see why this is so essential by envisioning a legal team without this quality. If team members are routinely concerned that their opinions will be ignored, mistakes berated, and questions judged as a reflection of lack of competence, what happens next? Most lawyers in this situation would retreat to self-protection: "I'm just going to keep my head down and focus on *my* work." Because they are treated like cogs in a machine, they act like cogs in a machine, meaning they do only the minimum necessary to get their tasks done successfully. Nothing more, nothing less.

This is the "stay in your lane" mentality, and lawyers fall into this trap at every level, from junior associates who just want to avoid ruffling a senior associate's feathers to partners who want nothing to do with internal politics. Attorneys focused on self-protection do not think, "How can I make the firm or practice group better?" Such a mentality would require taking on risks, including engaging in difficult conversations, providing feedback, or making suggestions that might be rejected. In this type of dis-couraging environment, the stay-in-your-lane mentality becomes the norm, attorneys clock in and out like a factory, and turnover rates rise while innovation and autonomy wane.

Hopefully, the problem is becoming obvious. Attorneys who stay in their lane, by definition, focus on their tasks, not the prac-tice's broader goals. They don't contribute to making the team itself better. They don't volunteer peer feedback, much less upward feedback. They want to perform well, but only to the extent that it boosts their career trajectory, not because they feel a sense of genuine commitment to the firm or the client. And because they focus on doing "what they are told," their managers must do an awful lot of "telling." Say goodbye to the vision of a team that doesn't need you every five minutes. Say hello to micromanagement.

This is why we need trust on our legal teams. Some people roll their eyes at the word "trust," thinking of trust falls, friendship bracelets, and other clichés. That is not the kind of trust we are seeking. In fact, we should clearly differentiate between personal and professional trust.

Professional trust—the kind of trust our teams need—is less about knowing the intimate details of one's personal life (although that kind of connection has value) and more about creating an environment where team members feel that others will support them, listen to their concerns, and respect their contributions, even if they occasionally make mistakes or step on someone's toes. In a professional environment, that kind of trust greases the machinery of collaboration. And I think we can all agree that a truly collaborative team beats a mere "collection of smart individuals" any day of the week.

THE ROLE OF VULNERABILITY

Before diving deeper, we need to cover an important prerequisite, one that will resurface over and over through the next several chapters. To unlock trust, leaders have to encourage—and model—vulnerability on their teams. This is a topic that makes many attorneys squirm in their seats, but it is necessary. Too often, leaders worry that vulnerability will be perceived as weakness. This derives from the assumption that leaders are supposed to have all the answers, meaning they should never question their own ideas, ask for help, or make (much less admit) mistakes. But that model of invulnerability sets up a hierarchical paradigm where psychological safety *cannot exist*.

Imagine a junior attorney on a team where the partner leading the team appears to be perfect in every way. The standard of the "perfect partner" implies that the junior associate's goal is to achieve that same pedestal of perfection. Admitting mistakes and asking for help would seem to reinforce how junior the associate is. Far better to err on the side of arrogance ("I already know the answer") or at least deference ("I'll do it exactly how you showed me") rather than admit weakness ("I could use some help here"). When an attorney's job is simply to execute the will of the impeccable partner, the attorney is once again reduced to a minion, just hoping to survive long enough to take a place at the top of that hierarchy (or burning out long before getting there).

On the contrary, when senior attorneys model and lead from a place of vulnerability—admitting mistakes, apologizing, asking questions, seeking help—mutual trust is not only possible, it's *inevitable*. This type of leadership builds a deep level of respect, boosts confidence in junior associates, and demonstrates an honest openness to feedback.

This attitude also reflects a level of authenticity that today's lawyers crave in a leader. Attorneys want to work for human beings, not demigods. Those late nights working together to hit a deadline, back against the wall, making tough calls despite imperfect information—these are the kinds of moments that actually bring teams together. It is the messiness, the ambiguity, the knowledge that we do not know everything—these are the times when partners show themselves to be just as human and prone to imperfection as anyone else. And these moments of vulnerability build loyalty.

As we proceed through the next few chapters, keep these core principles in mind. In order to unlock trust on our teams, we need to encourage psychological safety, and to have psychological safety, we need vulnerability. Follow this path, and not only will we achieve trust, but we will also unlock access to the other traits of high-performance legal teams—ownership, productive conflict, and accountability—that await in the remainder of this book.

A RIGOROUS APPROACH TO TRUST

Many tend to assume that trust can only be built naturally, a little bit at a time, through shared spaces, projects, accomplishments, and failures. If you want to wait that long, be my guest. By the time you have built trust organically, your attorneys will have left for greener pastures.

Allowing trust to build organically is inefficient for modern legal teams, where attorneys have to parachute into new cases or deals and ramp up to maximum effectiveness as quickly as possible. And today, most teams have embraced some element of hybrid or remote work as part of COVID-19's post-pandemic reality, reducing the frequency of casual, face-to-face interactions that used to drive much of a team's culture. In other words, we cannot simply wait for trust to happen, given enough time. Managers, you are responsible for *making* it happen.

The chapters that follow will explain why trust is often elusive on legal teams and how to build strong bonds of trust that unlock more collaborative, more productive, and higher-retention teams.

First, we will explain the barriers to trust. As it turns out, our brains are wired in ways that make trust more difficult to form due to two common challenges that we will discuss next: the fundamental attribution error (Chapter 2) and working style differences (Chapter 3). Although these barriers have natural causes, they can be overcome with awareness and practice. This understanding can not only improve our teams but help in our efforts to reduce systemic inequality in our organizations.

Chapter 4 will then offer specific exercises attorneys can use to build trust on their teams. The kind of trust we need—genuine, professional trust—is built brick by brick, both through thoughtful one-on-one interactions and group activities designed to break down the barriers of trust discussed earlier and promote healthy bonds across team members.

We need this kind of rigorous roadmap because relying solely on our intuitions can only get us so far. In fact, as we'll see in the next chapter, our "gut instincts" can sometimes lead us in entirely the *wrong* direction. But to understand that, we have to back up a few million years.

CHAPTER 2

THE FUNDAMENTAL ATTRIBUTION ERROR

To understand the first barrier to trust on legal teams, a type of cognitive bias known as the fundamental attribution error, we need to return to the age of the dinosaurs.

In the early stages of our evolution, long before we resembled anything close to human, the parts of the brain that developed the most were those that were critical to physical survival. The section around the human brainstem, often called the "reptilian" brain because its origins date nearly that far back in our evolutionary family tree, helps control everything from respiration to cardiac functions to the fight-or-flight response.* This part of the brain does not "think"—at least not in the cognitive

---

* Although "fight or flight" has become a well-known abbreviation for this phenomenon, psychologists have expanded this concept over the years, sometimes calling it the "fight, flight, freeze, or fawn" response to account for other survival mechanisms. But we'll use the more colloquial name here.

way that we usually mean when we use that word. This part of the brain simply "does." It reacts quickly, almost automatically, to save us from threats.

Hear a tiger growling behind you? Your reptilian brain increases your heart rate to get blood pumping to your muscles, dilates your pupils so you can see threats even in low light, and releases adrenaline so you can move like the wind. This is your brain readying you to face the threat and—hopefully—survive it.

Fast forward to the present day. Humans' brains have evolved much further, but the reptilian brain is still with us, at the base of our skull, sending out impulses that the rest of our brain has to process and decide whether to act on or override. And this is where a host of cognitive errors, or biases, come into play.

One of these humans was Jack, a senior associate I advised a few years ago (and whose identity, like others in this book, has been altered for confidentiality). Jack, like so many homo sapiens I have worked with over the years, was not interested in talking about evolutionary psychology. He came to me asking how to deal with a junior associate he was supervising who was routinely missing internal deadlines on a case he worked on for Jack.

For example, the week prior, the associate was supposed to send draft language related to a motion to compel discovery on Tuesday. But Tuesday night, no email came. Wednesday morning: nothing. Finally, the draft showed up in Jack's inbox late Wednesday afternoon, and sections of it were still incomplete. Worse, this wasn't the first instance.

After he explained the problem, I asked Jack, "Why has the associate been missing those deadlines?"

Jack looked at me like I had just asked why apples fall from a tree. After hesitating a bit, he finally said, "I haven't asked him directly, but clearly he doesn't take these deadlines seriously. It's just disrespectful. I am going to sit him down and tell him that you can't blow off deadlines, even if they are just internal deadlines. That's just not going to fly here."

Some attorneys may sympathize with Jack's anger. In fact, some will not see any problem with Jack's proposed plan of action. Hold onto those thoughts; we'll break down a number of best practices for feedback in Chapter 16 that will illuminate several missteps here by Jack. For now, though, we will focus on a more fundamental issue with Jack's brain. Jack is frustrated with another attorney's behavior, and rather than consider the circumstances that may cause the associate to act this way, Jack assumes this is a problem with the associate himself: a lack of respect, or simply "not getting it," as though the associate does not have the basic competence to understand what a deadline is.

In other words, Jack sees a misstep in another associate's behavior, and instead of inquiring into the *circumstances*, he jumps to judgment about the *person*.

Could there be another explanation for the associate's missed deadlines? We could brainstorm several. Perhaps the associate was stretched across multiple matters and fell behind even after long nights at the office. Perhaps the associate knew about the deadline but thought an extra day would not be a problem, given the overall discovery timeline. Perhaps the associate believed it necessary to prioritize different deadlines and simply made a judgment call (and failed to communicate it to Jack). Or perhaps, despite Jack's insistence that he was clear about the deadline, Jack never actually communicated the deadline as concretely as he believed.

Instead of considering these possible explanations, each of which might be coachable, Jack jumped to a more critical judgment about the associate that left him throwing up his hands in frustration and offering a potentially condescending lecture. Rather than trust that the associate was intelligent and hard-working, Jack's speech would imply the associate needed to work harder and be "more respectful." Imagine how the associate would react to that. Would that increase psychological safety, or destroy it?

DEFINING THE ERROR

Jumping to judgment rather than inquiring into circumstances is precisely the kind of error attorneys make about colleagues all the time, and it is a perfect manifestation of the fundamental attribution error.

First, a definition. The fundamental attribution error refers to our tendency to believe that other people's actions are explained by their *character* (or competence or other personality traits), but we explain our own actions by pointing to the *circumstances*.

If that definition is a mouthful, consider a more routine example. Imagine you are driving home one afternoon when all of a sudden, the driver in front of you runs a red light. Your immediate response might be: *What a jerk!* (Actually, in response to this hypothetical in seminars, attorneys routinely shout our far more colorful responses.) But, minutes later, when *you* run a red light, you justify it. *I was running late. It had just turned yellow. At least I looked both ways!*

This bias in how we explain others' behavior is why this is called the fundamental attribution *error*: when others make mistakes, we attribute those mistakes to their having poor character—they are thoughtless, they are lazy, they are reckless—and their mistakes or shortcomings are reflections of who they are *as people*. But by contrast, when *we* make a mistake, we explain and excuse our actions as a function of extenuating *circumstances*.

This is precisely the error Jack was making. Based on the missed deadlines he observed, he concluded the junior associate lacked a basic understanding or appreciation for internal deadlines. How does one coach someone with such incompetence? Jack felt his best option would be a lecture on the importance of *not* missing deadlines. While I am all for "lighting a fire" in certain situations, Jack is far more likely to cause problems with this tactic than solve them.

Because Jack jumped straight to judging the junior associate's competence, instead of inquiring into the circumstances—a classic example of the fundamental attribution error—he found himself down a dead-end path with no constructive guidance. Many attorneys in this situation throw up their hands and might even complain to a peer about the problem, who will dutifully shrug in agreement and offer a dismissive "what can you do" response, implicitly endorsing their sense of helplessness.

But if the tables were turned and Jack was the one who had missed a few deadlines, he likely would hope that the person reviewing his work would know that he is a hard-working, careful attorney who probably had good reason for doing so. Whatever the explanation, Jack would hope that his boss would at least consider that such an explanation exists—that the circumstances, rather than his character or competence, are to blame.

It may not seem like it, but Jack's judgmental attitude is the reptilian brain at work. The same fight-or-flight response that helped us survive deadly encounters often prevents us from thinking more deeply about others' motivations. When you hear that tiger growling behind you, you are not going to stop and think about the tiger's side of the story. *Maybe he had a difficult day. Perhaps he has not had a meal in quite some time. Poor tiger probably needs a friend.*

Nonsense. Your reptilian brain is going to recognize a predator and trigger you to respond accordingly. No deeper thinking. Just reacting.

Cognitive shortcuts like these are quite useful in critical survival situations, but not so much in the courtroom or boardroom. Unfortunately, our brain is still wired with these neural pathways despite our elevation in the food chain. When faced with a stressor, a challenge, or virtually any situation where judgment is required, our brains rarely consider all possible information—at least not at first. Instead, our brains try to apply mental shortcuts wherever possible. Like the fight-or-flight response, the fundamental attribution error is one such mental shortcut; it allows for quick, even if sometimes incorrect, judgments. Shortcuts like these are wired into our psychology, and while they provide us many advantages over other species, they can also lead to destructive behavior between humans.

BUT WHAT'S THIS HAVE TO DO WITH TRUST?

Remember that trust requires psychological safety: the freedom to take risks and admit mistakes without fear of reprisal. The erroneous instinct to blame "the person" rather than inquire into "the circumstances" acts like a wedge between team members—and annihilates trust. If your team members judge your every misstep as a sign of your lack of competence, character, or commitment, then psychological safety cannot exist. That is not a team ready to have your back and support your growth as an attorney. And without that safety and support, you are less likely to go out of your way to help them as well. It's a dog-eat-dog world.

This may sound dramatic, but it is a common pattern in mismanaged teams. When team members' slipups immediately result in judgment rather than support, trust spirals. As a result, they become laser-focused on self-preservation instead of thinking about the good of the team, the case, or the client.

REWIRING THE BRAIN

The erroneous impulse to judge another's character before considering the circumstances may be hard-wired into our brains, but that doesn't mean we need brain surgery to fix it. We simply need to be more aware of this impulse and learn not to rely on it so heavily. It turns out that if people are educated about the fundamental attribution error and coached to recognize it, they learn to reduce its impact on their thinking. This is an essential part of self-awareness, but this learning doesn't just "happen" naturally.

It all starts with an assumption of *good intentions*. If we assume others have good intentions, accusations of bad behavior are replaced by genuine curiosity. *"Why did he do that?"* shifts from being an angry, rhetorical accusation into a genuine question.

This is an action that costs you very little: a few seconds to reflect on your instinctual response—e.g., frustration, anger, character assumptions—and a few seconds to consider other plausible options for the person's behavior. This reframing becomes more natural with practice, particularly as the negative emotions that surround the fundamental attribution error dissipate and trust becomes more apparent.

In my seminars, for example, I propose a series of basic hypotheticals where snap judgments are common and invite participants to consider plausible positive intentions behind the behavior.

Let's start with an easy one:

Hypothetical #1: A Colleague Is Late For a Meeting

What positive (or at least, neutral) intentions might explain such behavior? Instead of assuming this person is unreliable or rude, we could imagine plenty of reasons for the lateness that have nothing to do with the person's character: traffic, responding to an urgent client request, a prior meeting running over, and so on. Simple enough.

Next, an intermediate example:

Hypothetical #2: A Colleague Interrupts You

Everyone has had the experience of being cut off in a conversation. Sometimes, it rolls off your back. Other times, it makes your nostrils flare. (Which is, by the way, part of the fight-or-flight response. Wider nostrils allow in more oxygen, which helps our bodies move faster when dealing with a predator. Lizard logic, once again.) But rather than assume the person is disrespecting your ideas, with a moment of reflection, you can imagine many reasons for such an interruption. The person may have an urgent point, or may simply be excited about an idea, or may be trying to subtly tell you that you are going off track and wasting time. You might not like the execution, but there still may be a good intention behind what you encounter.

By now you see the pattern: we are assuming positive intent, which paves the way for curiosity, rather than accusation. Note that we are not making excuses for others' behavior; we are simply refusing to jump to conclusions about their character *without more information.*

Now a final, more advanced example:

Hypothetical #3: A Boss Micromanages You

Most attorneys have experienced micromanagement at some point, and the phenomenon is not restricted to junior associates. Even senior partners occasionally feel micromanaged, whether by the heads of their firm or clients second-guessing their work. It can feel like an attack on your autonomy, the equivalent of saying you are not trusted to do your job. There is no better way to sap the morale right out of even the highest performers.

It may be tempting to throw up one's hands in this situation and complain that the attorney is a "bad manager." But that is the fundamental attribution error talking. Instead, consider what positive intent might be behind this management behavior.

All the micromanagers I have even seen have had one thing in common: they care deeply about getting the work *done right.* In fact, I have never seen a micromanager who did not genuinely care about the quality of the team's output. That intention is not only positive, it's downright praiseworthy. It's the execution that is problematic.

Once you view the person this way, the problem seems more approachable. Instead of writing off the attorney as a "micromanager," as though the label is some kind of immutable character flaw, you instead see them as having good intentions and needing some help with tactics. By ignoring the siren call of the fundamental attribution error, you can enter the situation more open-minded and ready to help the manager improve, as opposed to approaching the conversation angry and ready to lash out—a career-limiting move.

FROM DIATRIBE TO DIALOGUE

Assuming *positive intent* of team members is the first step in over-coming the fundamental attribution error. By assuming your team members are smart, capable people, you no longer act on the temptation to lecture them or leap to negative judgments. Instead, you are ready to engage in something more construc-tive: genuine dialogue. The tone of such a conversation will be far more supportive and lend itself to a culture of trust.

For example, with micromanagers, you might acknowledge their earnest desire for quality work. You might then ask them what they were trying to accomplish when they engaged in cer-tain behaviors. (*Really* asking, not just rhetorically asking the question as though delivering a flippant cross-examination.) For example: "I noticed you dictated precise language for the client email, as opposed to asking for ideas. Were you doing that for efficiency? Were you worried about particular language?" Then you can have a meaningful conversation about the pros and cons of those tactics like two colleagues trying to figure out this "man-agement thing" together, rather than talking "at" the person like you are scolding a child.

When I suggested this approach to Jack in dealing with his junior associate's missed deadlines, he—like many attorneys in coaching—started off skeptical that my advice on the fundamen-tal attribution error had any practical value to his situation. After all, with something so basic as deadlines, wouldn't asking "why" simply come off as condescending?

Yes and no. Once you correct for the fundamental attribution error, you do not necessarily have to follow a script of asking, "Why did you do that?" Asking it that way may still come off accusatory.

Remember, the goal is to shift your mindset to one where you (a) assume positive intent, and (b) demonstrate genuine curiosity about those intentions and the person's process. Only then can you ensure that the conversation demonstrates trust.

For example, Jack could say, "I noticed the last two provisions you were working on came in a day or two after our internal deadline. We still got the deal done, but it left me scrambling a bit to incorporate your work. Can you walk me through what happened?" Or better yet, inject empathy, e.g., "I know you have a lot on your plate, and sometimes these deal timelines can be downright grueling. How are you managing your priorities? How can I help?"

We will dive deeper into feedback later, including frameworks to structure difficult conversations, but the point is that none of these conversations will be constructive unless you overcome the fundamental attribution error and assume positive intent. Judgments about others make us feel superior, which can be emotionally satisfying in the moment, but they also lead to a "me versus them" mentality that prevents genuine collaboration.

THE POWER OF ASSUMING POSITIVE INTENT

When concerned about another attorney's work or behavior, the assumption of positive intent orients us to approach the situation constructively, but it does not mean the person is "off the hook." There may be situations in which an attorney's work falls so far below the standard expected in their role that a performance improvement plan or formal departure is warranted. Or there may be situations where an attorney's behavior, either at work or outside of work, crosses a line that cannot be tolerated.

The assumption of good intent does not foreclose these possibilities; it is simply a starting point for inquiry that in no way binds your hands from taking more severe action later. Assuming positive intent is not a "get out of jail free" card. If anything, it is more akin to "innocent until proven guilty."

Assuming good intentions may sound vague or cliché, but it is critical. As this book progresses, many of the tools we will use will become more and more concrete. But we have to start at the bottom, with the fundamentals. And nothing is so fundamental as the fact that we are dealing with human beings, with human flaws.

Finally, be warned that assuming positive intent is more difficult than it sounds. In fact, it can be absolutely exhausting, especially when you feel like the other person in the situation does not return the favor. Even if you perfect this skill, you may find yourself frustrated that *you* are always the one who seems to take the high road when others do not. At times, you might find all this "people stuff" downright overwhelming.

To that, I say: welcome to the big leagues. If you plan to become a successful attorney merely through your brilliant legal knowledge, you are in for a bumpy career. To your left and right are other, well-qualified, hard-working attorneys who are every bit as insightful in their legal analysis. If you want to stand out, and if you want to deliver real value, you need to learn how to build incredible teams that love to work with you. Do that, and you can command any career path you choose. Dismiss the "people stuff" as rudimentary and beneath you, and your performance reviews may soon start with: "Great individual contributor, *but*..." That "but" is the sound of your career hitting a ceiling.

The fundamental attribution error is just one barrier to trust. But a second barrier—working style differences—can be even more subtle and thus more difficult to overcome. In the next chapter, we'll discuss how these differences manifest on legal teams, and why they so often get in the way of trust.

CHAPTER 3

WORKING STYLE DIFFERENCES

I won't sugarcoat this one: Greg and Lisa despised each other. They were associates on a team that was struggling, which is how I came into the picture. As a strategic advisor, I was asked to investigate, and it took very little time to see that the frayed relationship between Greg, a senior associate, and Lisa, a junior associate, was not only making them both miserable; it was dividing the team (of more than a dozen lawyers) into factions. It took just two people to turn an entire team toxic.

I met privately with Greg and Lisa, and they readily unloaded their frustrations. Greg complained that Lisa was not committed to the team, lacked structured thinking, and was disorganized. Greg was convinced that Lisa was simply not pulling her weight. On the other hand, Lisa complained that even though she worked long hours and hit her goals, it was "never enough" for Greg. He did not support or mentor her, was not interested in her as a person, and simply expected her to clock in and clock out, deliver work product, and respond to emails without complaint.

Whatever you might think based on these mutual accusations, this was not a situation where either Greg or Lisa lacked talent. In fact, it was obvious to me and the practice group leader that they were two high performers, at least in terms of their individual work contributions. Even though they had the raw skills required to be effective as attorneys, they *could not* work together. At every step along the way, they had friction. They bickered in team meetings and complained about the other privately to their own trusted colleagues (who, it should be said, did little to address the situation productively—a topic for a later chapter).

In other words, Greg and Lisa lacked any shred of trust.

You might be thinking that this is simply another example of the fundamental attribution error at work. You are correct, but there was something else going on here as well. For all intents and purposes, Greg and Lisa, despite speaking the same language, growing up in the same city, attending the same college (yes, really), and having plenty of interests in common, were essentially aliens to one another. Beneath their superficial similarities was a gulf of difference. Their civil war came down to differences in *working styles*. In this chapter, we will explore different types of working styles and how, if not recognized and addressed, they can undermine trust and consume a team.

SEPARATING STYLES FROM SUBSTANCE

Successful attorneys often make the mistake of assuming that "their way" is the right way.

At the beginning of my legal career, I remember sitting in one of the firm's largest conference rooms attending a trial skills training run by a partner famous for his courtroom talents. I personally revered that partner and was enthusiastic about the subject matter; I was part of a national champion mock trial team in college, so this training was like I'd died and gone to nerd heaven. But by the end of the training, I found myself brutally disappointed.

It wasn't that he lacked the talent. Far from it; when he did demonstrations and mock examinations, it was like watching a wizard at work. The problem was that this was a training seminar, not a TV show. He wasn't teaching us how to be great trial lawyers; he was teaching us how to be like *him*. He only knew how to teach us *his* style, with all his quirks and flamboyance. This implied that his way was the only way—the best way. But it was only the best way for him. Entertaining? Absolutely. Educational? Not particularly.

This same spectacle also plays out routinely in how many attorneys manage their teams. Their preferences on communication, on responsiveness, on project management, and more, are all that matter. *They* dictate what good looks like, and those who do not fit the mold are considered, well, misfits.

But differences in working styles are entirely normal and should not be confused with gaps in competency or effectiveness. If attorneys do not learn to make this distinction, then not only will firms and organizations lose genuinely high performers, but they will also end up promoting only people who look, think, write, speak, and act in a similar way. This is one of many reasons that law firms and other organizations struggle with diversity—not because of malicious intent, but because of the subtle forces that lead managers to reward team members that are mirror images of themselves.

These types of differences come in many forms: personality differences, communication differences, social differences, and more. If you have taken a personality assessment like the

Myers-Briggs Type Indicator, DiSC, or Enneagram, then you are familiar with how these assessments can reveal much about you and increase your self-awareness. But they can also help us understand why we have friction with some team members and how to build stronger teams that can navigate these differences.

In this chapter, we will explore a type of assessment called Social Styles which, although its name might suggest otherwise, is directly relevant to how we work. This assessment has been around for decades, and its simplicity makes it uniquely suited to our goals. Attorneys need to be able to identify and adapt to differences in working styles quickly, without asking everyone in the office to take a 60-minute personality test. Social Styles theory serves that purpose well: there are just four styles to understand, and they are generally easy to spot "in the wild" without a degree in psychology. Most importantly, their impact on how we manage our teams will quickly become obvious.

If you are inspired by this topic and want to dive deeper, by all means, take the Myers-Briggs Type Indicator or Enneagram for a more nuanced look at yourself (and others). But for now, Social Styles will provide us the key lessons we need about how working styles can affect our teams.

THE BASICS OF SOCIAL STYLES THEORY

Social Styles theory was developed by two psychologists, David Merrill and Roger Reid, in the 1960s.* Even without taking a

---

* Merrill went on to found a company, TRACOM, that commercialized the research. I have no affiliation with TRACOM, but they offer a wealth of resources for purchase, if appropriate for your budget.

formal Social Styles assessment, the basics are easy to understand. The goal here is not to make you an expert in Social Styles; instead, the goal is to walk away with concrete examples of how the nuances of personality differences can have a tangible impact on how we work together as attorneys—and how to leverage that insight to become better team members and leaders.

SOCIAL STYLES OVERVIEW

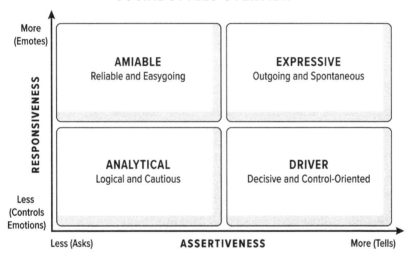

In the above diagram, you will see four Social Styles laid out on a simple two-axis chart. The styles are determined based on two scores: one for assertiveness (x-axis) and one for responsiveness (y-axis). In this context, a highly "assertive" person is direct and intentional, more goal-oriented, and wants control of a situation, while someone with a lower degree of assertiveness will ask more questions, be more patient, and listen. A person who is highly "responsive" is more in touch with their emotions, prioritizing personal connections and stories rather than just facts and logic; a less responsive person might find emotional engagement tedious or excessive and will put personal conversations off until after the work is done. I am oversimplifying, but these basic differences should be easy to imagine.

As you glance at this grid, you may be able to identify yourself (or some colleagues) fairly quickly. We will discuss each personality type in detail with the intention of identifying the one that resonates most closely with you *in a work environment*. That said, it is rare to fit perfectly into one of these categories. You may have aspects of multiple types. In other words, you are not trying to put yourself "in a box" but rather develop greater self-awareness about your natural style and tendencies.

Also, keep in mind that all of these styles have both positive and negative attributes, aspects that contribute to a person's success and qualities that can lead to shortcomings or misunderstandings. In fact, any person's strengths, when overused, can lead to their weaknesses. This is typical. There is no "right" or "wrong" social style, no matter your profession, as each social style adds value and diversity to a team.

Disclaimers complete. Now read about each style below and consider which aspects resonate the most with you.

The Analytical
Qualities: Logical // Cautious // Task-oriented
Basic need: To be right

An analytical person (or "an analytical" for short, which is how Social Style monikers are often treated) tends to approach situations methodically, assessing every angle before coming to an intentional conclusion. They ask questions persistently, homing in on details and facts, which can lead to missing social cues. Because they seek to be as well-informed as possible, it can take a while for them to make a decision. And once they've made a decision, they stick to it—sometimes stubbornly—because they already believe they've considered all sides. In a conflict, the analytical person might become dismissive, sarcastic, or negative.

You can spot an analytical person in a meeting by their love of structure. They generally speak in lists, e.g., "there are three problems we need to address," or "we could go in one of two directions." When they are not ready to make a call, they will ask for more data, which can serve as a way of putting off a difficult decision. Finally, watch for them to start meetings focused on the task—meaning analyticals will not be as likely to spend the first five minutes of a meeting sharing weekend plans. Colleagues are more likely to describe analytical types as "serious" in work situations.

The Driver
Qualities: Decisive // Control-oriented // Goal-focused
Basic need: Results

Drivers tend to want every situation to be under control. They do not necessarily need to be in charge, but if a meeting starts to go off the rails, you may see them visibly frustrated, and they may even take over personally to right the ship—regardless of whether it is their meeting. Drivers relish the opportunity to marshal people and resources toward a common objective, and they tend to stay laser-focused on their goals. Because drivers value efficiency, they tend to look for shortcuts and make quick decisions, even if this sometimes entails skipping over details others think are important. Direct, active, and deliberate, the driver is willing to take risks and, in some cases, may inadvertently steamroll others who are in disagreement or slow to respond. Because drivers focus on tasks first (and people second), they can be perceived as aggressive or cold in some situations.

In short, drivers tend to abhor chaos and inefficiency. If a driver feels time is being wasted, it can be hard to hide that displeasure. And like analyticals, drivers are more likely to be sociable only after the work is done.

The Amiable
Key qualities: Reliable // Easy-going // Relationship-driven
Basic need: Security

Amiables are focused on the interpersonal side of the equation: they prefer consensus over conflict and value listening over talking. They are loyal, personable, and patient in dealing with others. This means amiables often form trust with colleagues quite easily and tend to have a strong pulse on the team. Rather than being focused on expanding their own power, they seek an environment where everyone can thrive.

In some cases, amiables' focus on maintaining good relationships can lead to challenges. Their desire for security and peace makes them slower to take risks, and their commitment to relationships can cause them to waffle in their convictions or avoid confrontations because they genuinely value everyone's perspective and want the group to get along as much as possible. This can result in slow decision-making and impede a group's progress in some cases.

Amiables also tend to appreciate having clear instructions rather than being left to "figure it out" in ambiguous problem spaces. When given direct instructions, they follow them closely rather than interpret them in ways that might lead them astray. If they have questions, they are more likely to hold off on asking them until the end or may wait until the next opportunity to do so one-on-one rather than in front of the group, a stark contrast to analyticals, who are more willing to jump in to ask questions in the middle of a meeting.

The Expressive
Key qualities: Outgoing // Spontaneous // Enthusiastic
Basic need: Appreciation

Expressives enjoy the company of others because they seek an outlet to—no surprise here—"express" themselves. More likely to be described as the "life of the party" compared to other styles, expressives are enthusiastic, talkative, and "interesting," particularly because they become more engaged as they receive more attention.* Expressives are also more likely than other types to have visionary, outside-the-box ideas, with an optimistic outlook that sees endless possibilities.

In a meeting, the expressive person may not want to follow a strict agenda. Instead of getting in the weeds on facts and research, they might be "hooked" by a compelling story or narrative. They are also more likely to tell stories of their own, which can sometimes put drivers and analyticals on edge if they think the stories are a distraction from the topic at hand.

Expressives usually like things "big"—big stories, big picture, big ideas, and yes, often big emotions. They want to engage others

---

* You might be wondering if some styles coincide with introvert and extrovert tendencies. Not always. For example, I am a driver at heart with secondary tendencies on the analytical side. Despite these being task-oriented styles, I am a high-extrovert; I simply prefer to be social after the work is done because when I am engaged in a task, I tend to be hyper-focused on its completion. That said, if you would like to read more about introversion and extroversion, consider Susan Cain's perspective in her book, *Quiet: The Power of Introverts in a World That Can't Stop Talking* (New York: Crown, 2013).

and be engaged. This can make them inspiring. But expressives can also be unpredictable or prone to exaggeration. They can even become offended or uncollaborative under stress, perhaps requiring a bit more time to process their feelings and calm down after a difficult conversation.

PUTTING THE "SOCIAL" IN SOCIAL STYLES

As you read through the Social Styles, hopefully you picked up on a few areas that reflect your natural tendencies at work. You may have found yourself putting your colleagues in imaginary Social Style boxes as well. If not, go back through again with that goal in mind, because comparing your style to that of your colleagues is where this gets interesting.

It turns out that many conflicts at work are caused not by gaps in competence or capability but by clashes in Social Styles. These style differences add friction to everyday interactions and make it harder to build trust.

Let's return to Greg and Lisa. These two attorneys could not have been more extreme examples of their Social Styles. Greg was a driver: decisive, control-oriented, structured, and motivated. His primary focus was on getting the work done, and any attention spent on frivolous conversation topics (like "how was your weekend") suggested, to him, a lack of focus. When Greg set his mind to a goal, he crushed it, and his ruthless efficiency made him a star among his peers, which is why he was given management responsibilities.

On the other hand, Lisa was an expressive, driven by the desire to connect with people first. She had a strong work ethic, but she wasn't the type to start every meeting with a six-point agenda. She felt a more organic approach allowed for better creativity and collaboration. When Greg gave her directions, she felt it was important to adapt those directions to her situation, and she did not want to report every little deviation back to Greg, since she thought she should be trusted to get the job done. But her biggest frustration was with Greg's cold approach to management. She consistently tried to bond with Greg, but even her most basic attempts at small talk at the beginning of a meeting were met with stonewalling, and he never once asked her about her life outside of work.

As a result of this clash of styles, Greg thought Lisa was disorganized, not focused on work, and unwilling to respect his authority. Meanwhile, Lisa thought Greg was a robotic micromanager with no interest in actually developing (or even getting to know) his team.

In short, Greg and Lisa each believed the other was ineffective and would not waver. Rather than see their friction as a result of differences in their working styles, which they could have acknowledged and potentially accommodated, they each simply chalked the problems up to the other's lack of competency and capability. Attorneys who fall into this trap destroy value—and potentially, careers.

In some ways, this is an extension of the lesson from the last chapter about the fundamental attribution error. But Social Styles offer something even more concrete: they offer a cheat sheet for building trust with colleagues more effectively—that is, if you are willing to throw out the Golden Rule.

THE PLATINUM RULE

We all grew up hearing that we should treat others as we would like to be treated. This turns out to be terrible management advice. In fact, it is why so many junior associates who complain about their managers nevertheless turn out to be problematic managers themselves. They think they have spotted flawed management in action and have the solutions ready in their minds, only to find out the hard way that their preferred approaches do not necessarily work for others.

When we treat people how we want to be treated, we force our styles—including our needs, motivations, communication patterns, and more—onto them. If you find your manager's style frustrating, and then you turn around and manage a team of people "the way you would want to be managed," you can bet that many—if not most—of your team members will find your style off-putting in some ways. After all, from the perspective of Social Styles theory, you have only a roughly one-in-four chance of your direct report sharing your working style, and even this fails to take into account other personality dimensions not captured by Social Styles theory. (The Myers-Briggs Type Indicator provides for sixteen different personality styles spread across the population. As an "ENTJ," for example, only about 2% of people share my particular personality cocktail.)

Great management requires treating others the way *they* want to be treated as much as possible. Sometimes called "the platinum rule," this necessitates not only a deep sense of self-awareness—of our own preferences, tendencies, and fallacies—but also an intelligent understanding of our team members' personalities and approaches.

HOW WORKING STYLES IMPEDE TRUST

When we do not consider others' styles, we make it more difficult to build trust with colleagues. Imagine an expressive attorney comes into a meeting and pitches the team on a new litigation strategy. It's bold, and it's not without risk, but if successful, it could put the other side on their heels. The expressive attorney is visibly excited, grinning like a kid with a shiny new toy.

How will an "analytical" colleague react? Likely instant skepticism. The analytical attorney wants to understand the thought process step by step and has a host of objections to address before even considering this left turn. But even if the expressive attorney already thought through all of these objections, the attorney may still dismiss the analytical's questions as tedious—missing the forest for the trees—and become defensive, perhaps accusing the analytical of lacking vision. In response, the analytical may point to this accusation as yet another example of the expressive attorney's "tornado" style: coming into a meeting, dropping a bombshell without thinking it through, and leaving it to the team to pick up the pieces.

Much like the previous chapter, we again have a situation where people jump to negative conclusions rather than consider other factors. But unlike the fundamental attribution error, which refers to underestimating the value of the *circumstances* in explaining behavior, here, we are concerned with misunderstandings about how *personality traits* affect behavior.

Personality traits can and do affect how we behave at work. They manifest as differences in working styles, and if attorneys are not careful, they will make the mistake of judging colleagues based on whether the colleague behaves the same way *they* would in that situation. When people do things a different way than we would, we tend to jump to the conclusion that what they are doing is suspect—and subpar. Differences spark distrust. This is another example of a mental shortcut; our brains try to make judgments quickly, and it is easier to assume that "different" is "bad." This is why snap judgments reduce psychological safety and erode trust.

Instead of jumping to conclusions, the analytical audience member should have considered whether differences in working styles may be responsible for the clash, rather than differences in competency, and approached the situation with a more open mind. Unlike the fundamental attribution error discussed in the last chapter, however, a clash of working styles represents a two-way street. Just as the audience member can avoid jumping to conclusions, the presenter could also have adapted the message to the audience and avoided the clash altogether. We will explore those techniques next.

ADAPTING TO OTHERS' WORKING STYLES

As a strategic consultant, I often find myself working with team leaders who are trying to determine how best to frame their work to the CEO or another executive. Rather than just say, "Think about your audience," as though that clichéd advice immediately shines a light in the darkness, I offer a few basic questions to guide them to the best approach, such as:

- Does your stakeholder start with small talk or save the chit-chat until the work is done?
- Does your stakeholder like diving into the weeds or find details tedious?
- Does your stakeholder speak in structures (e.g., "I see three options") or prefer to deliver more of a stream of consciousness?
- Does your stakeholder need time to digest new information or jump right in with questions and opinions?

These questions reflect differences in Social Styles. Even if you do not have an extensive relationship with the stakeholder, you usually have enough information to make some educated guesses. Then you can think about the best way to approach the conversation. This can allow you to land points better with colleagues— and even clients.

For example, below is a chart with tips on how to adapt to your counterpart's Social Style. Before reading through the list, imagine a boss, colleague, or client that you sometimes struggle to convince. Then consider if these tips might make it easier to connect with that person.

TIPS FOR WORKING WITH ANALYTICALS

- Sit side-by-side to focus them on the problem, not the person, e.g., together in front of a whiteboard or screen
- Structure ideas into lists and outlines
- Explain thought processes, e.g., factors you considered, what research you did that got you to this conclusion, or how you gathered your data
- Build your argument based on evidence and data, not storytelling
- Clearly cite sources and be prepared to answer probing questions about them
- Avoid emotional appeals

TIPS FOR WORKING WITH DRIVERS

- Provide clear agendas and be explicit about the goals for the meeting or the decisions you want to resolve
- Come with proposals, not just questions

- For complex topics, include an executive summary upfront with key insights and recommendations
- Stay in control when meetings get derailed by either explicitly altering the agenda to include the topic or tabling it until later
- End with clear action items, including names and deadlines for each

TIPS FOR WORKING WITH AMIABLES

- Ease into controversial topics, making clear you are open to feedback
- Provide a pre-read to ensure time for the amiable to prepare thoughts
- When supervising an amiable, be more detailed with instructions and clear expectations
- Create space for questions and directly ask for their input/ feedback
- Allow time to process, especially with complex subjects, e.g., circling back the next day to check for lingering questions or concerns
- Thank them for ideas and feedback

TIPS FOR WORKING WITH EXPRESSIVES

- Allow time for personal connections and conversations, e.g., start with small talk
- Sit across from them, allowing plenty of eye contact
- Listen for and acknowledge personal stories
- Focus on the big picture
- Tell a story, rather than just dumping facts and data
- Avoid too much process

Notice how there is no universal approach that works for everyone, which is precisely the point. Everyone is different, and sometimes the best approach for one person might not be optimal for another. For example, it might be best to sit side by side with an analytical lawyer with papers or the laptop screen in front, which focuses the analytical's attention on the problem rather than squaring off with the person. But with an expressive, sitting across from each other might be preferable because it allows for a more human connection.

Similarly, if you go into a meeting with a driver and fail to set a clear agenda upfront—and stick to it—the driver will notice. You may even find the driver interrupts to reframe the purpose of the meeting, a sure sign that you have failed to earn credibility as the meeting leader. Drivers usually appreciate a meeting that moves swiftly from agenda item to agenda item like you are ticking checkboxes off a list; it shows a "getting things done" mentality and demonstrates you are in command of the situation. And since the driver is rarely shy about asking questions, silence likely indicates you have the person's support.

But this same approach with an amiable will cause problems. The agenda itself is useful to provide direction, but if you move too quickly through the agenda, your "command of the situation" will instead read as dominance (or worse, arrogance) and crowd out the amiable's willingness to participate. You might leave the meeting thinking you have consent to move forward with your plan, but the amiable is actually harboring concerns or questions. Later, you will pay the price. You might then find yourself frustrated that you are relitigating an issue that you thought was already resolved, whereas from the amiable's perspective, you steamrolled the situation and never had true buy-in in the first place.

THE CHAMELEON CONCERN

Some of the attorneys I work with find this adaptive approach concerning. Why should they have to adapt to everyone else's style like some kind of color-changing chameleon? Isn't that inauthentic? And aren't there times when you want to counter someone's style rather than lean into it?

First, adapting to one's audience is a part of our toolkit as attorneys. From trial advocacy to deal-making to client management, we are constantly in situations where we have to get others on board with our ideas. The best way to do this is to think from the other side's perspective. Attorneys who do not get caught up in their own narratives and instead can put themselves in others' shoes often outperform their peers in almost every aspect of their jobs. This is one way to separate good from great when recruiting talent.

It is also true that people value authenticity—in their leaders, their colleagues, their bosses, and certainly their lawyers. But adaptation and authenticity are not incompatible. Rethinking a meeting's structure, for example, does not require "pretending to be someone you are not." Similarly, in some situations, attorneys accustomed to being direct might try a lighter touch, or those who are usually conflict-averse might try being a bit more direct. These are examples of pushing outside one's comfort zone, not upending one's personality. The more you push yourself, the more expansive your interpersonal toolkit becomes. But new tools do not change who *you* are. As long as you are honest with yourself and others, you can maintain your authenticity even as you find new ways to express yourself.

As to the last question, yes, it is wise to consider how you can avoid getting caught in traps caused by someone else's style. For example, if you work with an expressive attorney who relies heavily on narrative, that attorney may have blind spots around executional details. But to help them see both parts of the equation, I would suggest first starting with narrative—that is, meet them on their level—and then incorporating a section on execution into the story so that you can smoothly pivot into those matters, as opposed to sharply cutting off their thought process and redirecting their attention to yours.

The chameleon concern is understandable, and at the end of the day, there are no hard-and-fast rules about how and when to adapt to a colleague's style. It is as much art as science. But by and large, the more willing you are to consider the other side's perspective, the more successful you will be in building trust through productive conversations with your team members.

SYSTEMIC BARRIERS

The way we work is driven by much more than just personality traits. Gender identity, race, accessibility, background, geography, and much more can affect how people work in a team, including the way they deal with conflict, whom they go to for advice and feedback, their way of running meetings, and whether they are comfortable admitting mistakes.

Many years ago, a well-meaning CEO told me, "I don't see color or gender. I just judge people based on their work. We don't tolerate discrimination here." For him, that was the beginning and the end of the conversation.

Unfortunately, this approach, while well-intentioned, does not achieve fair outcomes. Simply codifying a policy against discrimination does not stop individual and systemic biases from taking their toll on law firms and other organizations. The data supporting this proposition is overwhelming, and I hope that most attorneys reading this have already taken this lesson to heart without me needing to justify it further. (The American Bar Association offers a wealth of research-backed articles tracking these trends.*) But I want to focus on a practical challenge that many attorneys have in creating a workplace free of bias. It is a challenge I face as well, despite my own "good intentions."

When we interact with our colleagues at work, we only experience a sliver of who they are; we do not see the lifetime of unique experiences that have shaped the people before us, experiences that contribute to our differences. If we do not account for differences, we will more than likely reward people who look and act the same as those in leadership, which in law firms tends to mean white men. Take me, for example: a white, cisgender, able-bodied male from a middle-income family. Wherever I went—at home, at school, or at work—I expressed my opinions freely, even to authority figures, who generally appreciated and rewarded my ideas, building my confidence (among a host of other privileges[7]). These experiences throughout my life make me comfortable today telling a manager my true thoughts and opinions.

If I expect everyone I work with to provide me with this same level of candor, then I am more likely to find myself connecting with and rewarding people who have a similar background to mine. This is a form of unconscious bias. Instead, as a leader, I need to understand that people have different life experiences and be prepared to coach and support my team members in different ways.

---

* The ABA has consolidated many of these resources through its Diversity and Inclusion Center. See *www.americanbar.org/groups/diversity* for more information.

This is one of the reasons why law firms have struggled with diversity and the retention of women and people of color, even when they genuinely want to avoid that outcome. It is difficult to be aware of, let alone correct for, all the subtle ways our team culture can include or exclude certain people. As scale, these individual behaviors can coalesce into genuine, systemic barriers.

I want to dive a bit deeper here and share a thought-provoking insight from the research of linguist Deborah Tannen. For those who have not read her bestselling book, *You Just Don't Understand: Women and Men in Conversation*, her research revealed a common pattern that differentiates how many men and women speak:

> For most women, the language of conversation is primarily a language of rapport: a way of establishing connections and negotiating relationships...For most men, talk is primarily a means to preserve independence and negotiate and maintain status in a hierarchical social order.[8]

In other words, Tannen's research found that women in conversation often look for ways to show they are members of the group, that they are "in" rather than "out." Sharing stories that demonstrate commonality help achieve this. Men, by contrast, tend to share stories that establish "status," perhaps even one-upping each other. Yes, these generalities can be dangerous—and Tannen's work is not without controversy—but since reading her book, I have seen this pattern play out over and over again both inside and outside of work.

One such example occurred a few years ago when I was COO and General Counsel at a technology company. Our company had recently been acquired by a private equity firm, and our executive team and a few senior members of the PE firm met for a celebratory dinner after a board meeting. Because of last-minute travel conflicts, not everyone could participate; it ended up being almost all men at the table.

At some point, one of the PE leaders shared a story about a time when he had been, of all things, a judge at a hot dog eating contest and nearly botched the job (to count consumed hot dogs) because he got distracted by another contestant. This prompted our CEO to share an opinion on the best hot dogs, which prompted a board member to share a story about the best mustard, which then prompted someone to talk about the best relish. They went in a circle for nearly ten minutes eagerly shouting over each other to compete for superlatives on hot dog toppings. Male bonding at its finest!

Would this same conversation have happened with a group dominated by women? Perhaps, but Tannen's research suggests it is less likely. Strutting for dominance in conversation tends to happen more often in male-centric groups. For a group with more women than men, stories about a mistake in judging a contest might have triggered stories about similar mistakes, not to one-up each other but to demonstrate common experience. Or conversations about condiments might focus more on acknowledging each person's suggestions (e.g., "that sounds amazing" and "I'll have to try that") rather than competing for who knows the best, most obscure deli mustard in New England.

Again, I recognize the danger in overextending or weaponizing these observations. Identifying common sociological patterns can be informative but can also trigger confirmation bias and inappropriate stereotypes. Personally, I don't always gravitate toward stereotypical, male-dominated conversation topics—you can forget about asking me if I saw the game last night, because I didn't—and I know plenty of female colleagues that have no trouble holding their own in (or even leading) the most aggressive boys' clubs. We know these traits are fluid.

But my point is simply that these subtle conversation differences can be yet another brick in the walls between colleagues. While many men would be comfortable jumping into the condiment round-robin, some women would not, instead finding the conversation absurd or off-putting. That little bit of extra friction, when you scale it across all the daily interactions we have with our colleagues, can create genuine barriers to connection and trust.

In other words, little things add up to big things. Differences based on gender, race, background, income, physical ability, and other aspects affect our work because they often come with different life experiences. I, for one, have never feared my ideas would be dismissed because of my skin color, but nearly all of my Black colleagues have shared that experience, and it shapes some of their approaches at work, regardless of how many leaders at their firms or organizations tout diversity. This book only scrapes the surface of these important topics. For a nuanced discussion about race and intersectionality backed by rich statistics (and life experience), consider *So You Want to Talk about Race*, by Ijeoma Oluo.[9] Or consider books by Jennifer Brown, such as *Inclusion: Diversity, the New Workplace & the Will to Change*.[10]

This is not a soapbox; this is practical guidance for anyone trying to build strong legal teams. The case for making our industry more inclusive is compelling for many reasons, from the importance of social justice to the fact that diverse teams actually *perform* better. Studies show that such teams consider more varied perspectives and generate sharper discussions, which results in them being more strategic, more rigorous in their decision-making, more innovative, and even more efficient, making decisions faster with fewer meetings.[11] And high-performance legal teams require trust, which develops more easily among attorneys who look, think, and talk the same way—a systemic (even if unconscious) bias. If you do not acknowledge and correct for this bias, then the attorneys on your team who will feel the most at ease, get the most support, and stick around the longest will likely be those cut from the same cloth as you. This is true regardless of your identity, but for attorneys from overrepresented groups, the impact of ignorance is particularly damaging because inertia tends to favor those already in majority positions.

For those of you managing other attorneys, you have a responsibility to address these issues proactively. You have to put in the work. It is not optional. And increasingly, as you progress in your career, your success will be judged based on *outcomes*, not simply whether you had the best of intentions.

Simply put: building trust across differences is part of the modern attorney's job description. Educate yourself, expand your network, and seek continuous feedback. You do not have to be perfect, but you do have to give these matters at least as much attention as you spend staying on top of the latest legal developments. Not only will you build stronger teams, but you will build stronger careers as well.

BEYOND THE BARRIERS

In the last two chapters, we have discussed barriers to trust, first with the fundamental attribution error and second with differences in working styles. Learning about these barriers, and how to avoid them, will have more impact when shared by the entire team, not just team leaders. When all team members become aware of the fundamental attribution error, take the time to understand their working styles, and acknowledge that there are different (and equally valuable) ways of working, psychological safety thrives. The result is a more trusting, more cohesive, more collaborative team.

Keeping these barriers in mind, we can next tackle the challenge of building trust *at scale*—that is, through exercises that work across an entire team, practice group, or firm.

CHAPTER 4

TRUST BUILDING WITHOUT TRUST FALLS

The concept of "trust-building" often conjures images of childhood summer camp: trust falls, ropes courses, and guitar sessions around the campfire. Those kinds of team bonding activities have their place and can be useful for creating social connections. But they will not be sufficient for building the kind of *professional* trust required for high-performance legal teams. We need a more rigorous, work-centric approach.

At one extreme, the United States military puts soldiers through an incredibly intense training process that forces individuals to learn to work together. Under high physical and mental stress, where accomplishing a goal is only possible through teamwork, soldiers learn they must rely on each other absolutely. When one of my peers—who later became a partner at a large law firm—returned from his second tour as a marine in Iraq, he said that while you try to always focus on the mission, at the end of the day, each soldier's true priority was the soldier next to him. Being there for a team member was what mattered most.

The military knows how to build strong teams. But it is hard to imagine mapping that process onto legal teams. We cannot rely on boot camps, physical stress, and life-and-death situations to imbue trust in team members. And while it is true that high-pressure situations like tight deadlines and heavy client demands can be trust-building experiences for lawyers, I do not recommend standing by and hoping that the stress of the job naturally acts as a pressure cooker.

Instead, we will discuss four exercises that can help team members build trust faster, even if they are new to the firm or the team.

EXERCISE #1: OPEN-ENDED CONVERSATIONS

After working with people for several years, you generally *know* them: their motivations and frustrations, their family members and hobbies, their working styles and goals. This knowledge—this organic intimacy—allows you to work more effectively with your colleagues. The question is: do you need to wait several years to learn all of this information by osmosis, or is there a more efficient way to pull this knowledge forward and expedite the effectiveness of your working relationships? The answer is yes—you can kick start this on day one, even—through thoughtful, open-ended questions.

During typical one-on-one sessions between attorneys, the focus is often entirely on the tasks at hand: the brief due tomorrow, the issues list for a transaction, and so on. While these tactical conversations are necessary (and certainly productive), they rarely leave time for broader issues, such as career development and relationship management. To build trust, attorneys should also be using one-on-ones once a month (or once a quarter) to demonstrate interest in the person's career, not just the task at hand. Deeper questions also invite vulnerability, which in turn reinforces psychological safety. Below is a list of questions to consider.

Open-Ended Questions to Build Trust

Motivations and Interests

- Why did you take this job? What motivates you to come into work every day?
- What type of work gives you the most energy? What feels exhausting or tedious?
- Which projects coming down our pipeline seem most appealing to you?
- How do you spend your time outside of work?

Growth and Goals

- What development areas are you currently working on? Are there specific skills you hope to build?
- What do you hope to achieve? What will that achievement unlock for you?
- If you left this job, what would the reason be?

Communication Style

- When are you generally available?
- How quickly will you typically respond to email? When should I follow up?

- Do you prefer questions by email, phone, or in-person? Do you like when people "pop in"?
- What does "EOD"/"COB" mean? (e.g., 5 p.m., 8 a.m. next business day, etc.)
- Will we conduct feedback sessions? How often? Do you expect two-way feedback?

Our Relationship
- What does it look like when you are under stress? How can others help?
- Think about your best team members or bosses. What made them stand out?
- What are some things I may not know about you?
- What drives you crazy? Pet peeves?

Where appropriate, make the conversation two-way, sharing a bit about yourself to even the playing field. Of course, you can spread these questions out over the course of many one-on-ones; you do not have to cover everything at once. But the sooner, the better. Not only will you gain useful information about how to work with this attorney more effectively, but you will earn more trust by showing you care enough to ask these questions.

Despite their trust-building value, some attorneys balk at asking these questions, either feeling that they are too invasive or too tedious. If it feels uncomfortable, lean into that and own it. For example, there is no harm in saying, "I read a book where the author recommended asking certain questions in one-on-ones. I know we've worked together a while, so this may seem silly. But I realized I have never actually asked you: What made you join [this firm/company]? What made you choose us over your last job?" Admitting something might be strange or awkward tends to break any such tension.

EXERCISE #2: "HOW TO WORK WITH ME" SLIDES

Thoughtful, open-ended questions can surface useful information for attorneys working together. But to take this concept a step further, consider having attorneys create a document or slide that answers some common questions about their style and preferences and storing them in the team's shared drive or folder.

For example, I worked with one client to build the template on the following page for their attorneys.

This idea was inspired by my time at Boston Consulting Group. There was a time at BCG when you could look up virtually any partner's "How to Work with Me" slide and instantly skip months of haphazard trial-and-error-based learning. These cheat sheets can be invaluable. You are welcome to download this template from www.allrisebook.com to use as a starting point. I recommend you tailor it to include information your team finds useful. Talk to a sample of attorneys on your team, get their reactions, and make adjustments as needed.

In my seminars with attorneys, some suggest that only leaders, such as partners and senior associates, should fill out these sheets for the benefit of more junior attorneys. They worry that asking everyone to complete the exercise implies that the partner will pander to the idiosyncratic styles of every junior associate. This concern is perhaps rational, but entirely impractical. I have never met a junior associate naive enough to think that filling out a sheet with communication preferences will translate into partners bowing to those preferences at every turn. And while I

IVAN IVERSON

MBTI: INTJ
Social Style: Amiable

BACKGROUND AND INTERESTS
- From Atlanta, Georgia
- 2 kids: Aubrey (5) and Bo (3)
- I love playing basketball. Hiking is a close second.

WORK PROFILE
- I learn primarily through discussion.
- I am very direct and may come off as too blunt, please tell me if this happens.
- I am very punctual; being late is a pet peeve.
- Please share your pet peeves with me so we can build a solid work relationship.

WORK STYLE
- It is critically important for me to understand the "big picture."
- I don't like to work late at the office.
- I usually start checking emails around 7:00 a.m. and stop around 11:00 p.m.
- My most productive hours are early in the morning.
- My least productive time is 4:30–6:30 p.m. I try to exercise during this time.
- I am unavailable during dinner hours on Friday evenings.
- My door is usually closed because I am listening to music, so please come in!
- I don't mind weekend emails; just be clear about deadlines and goals.
- I prefer concrete examples when receiving feedback.
- Be direct with me; I am not good with hints.

LEARNING AND TEACHING PREFERENCES

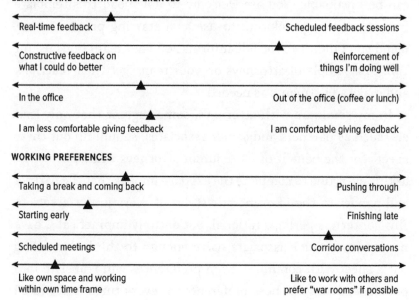

Real-time feedback | Scheduled feedback sessions

Constructive feedback on what I could do better | Reinforcement of things I'm doing well

In the office | Out of the office (coffee or lunch)

I am less comfortable giving feedback | I am comfortable giving feedback

WORKING PREFERENCES

Taking a break and coming back | Pushing through

Starting early | Finishing late

Scheduled meetings | Corridor conversations

Like own space and working within own time frame | Like to work with others and prefer "war rooms" if possible do not doubt that such a rare junior associate exists, we are not solving for that outlier.

But if partners are not going to adhere to junior associates' preferences, why bother asking for them?

Our goal is not to force one side to adapt to the idiosyncrasies of another. If you say to junior associates that only the partners have filled out "How to Work with Me" slides, we unnecessarily reinforce the image of partners as demigods and signal that junior associates' job is to bow to their individual whims. Junior associates already know partners are on top of the hierarchy; we do not need to double down. Doing so sends the wrong message and undermines our investment in building psychological safety. If anything, we want partners to seem more approachable, not less.

Instead, explain to them that the goal of building these cheat sheets is to increase transparency and skip over months or years of getting to know each other. Once we surface the information, we don't simply pick one set of preferences and act accordingly. We identify potential areas of conflict and talk through them.

For example, imagine a deal team where the partner likes to get back online at 9 p.m. after putting the kids to bed and work for another few hours, whereas the associate prefers to start work early and end by dinnertime. They could talk about the implications of these different styles. Perhaps the partner will say that the associate need not stay up until midnight, just in case an email comes in; any emails sent after 9 p.m. can wait until morning unless accompanied by a phone call. Or perhaps the associate will agree to check in at 10 p.m. on the eve of big deadlines, just in case something urgent requires overnight attention.

Without this two-way conversation—that is, if associates only saw the partner's working hours in a document with no opportunity for discussion and alignment—the associates might unnecessarily upend their otherwise reasonable lifestyle choices. Or the partners might be frustrated by associates' slow turnaround time, not realizing their team members simply had a different default schedule. These pain points are entirely avoidable, and showing you care enough to have this conversation dramatically increases trust.

EXERCISE #3: MOTIVATION SHARING

This next trust-building tool usually prompts a room full of eye rolls when I preview it during training sessions, but bear with me; in all the years I have been doing this exercise across all manner of audiences, I can honestly say even the harshest critics find it an eye-opening and genuinely powerful experience.

In a small group setting, such as breakout sessions of four to six attorneys each, go around in a circle and give everyone two to three minutes to answer this prompt:

What motivates you in work and in life? Explain your answer as it relates to your work today, then try to tie it back to your earliest memory (e.g., childhood) where this motivation manifested itself.

For participants who find the word "motivation" ambiguous, I provide a few examples to get their gears turning:

Examples: What motivates you in work and in life?
- **Justice**: I want to promote fairness and a level playing field
- **Mastery**: I want to develop deep expertise in a challenging field

- **Curiosity**: I want to learn something new every day
- **Problem Solving**: I want to tackle diverse new challenges
- **Impact**: I want to be a part of large-scale change in the world
- **Community**: I want to make a difference for those closest to me
- **Balance**: I want to work to live, not live to work
- **Competition**: I want to be at the top of my game
- **Something Else:** _____

Let's talk about the exercise from a pedagogical perspective. First, understanding team members' motivations has genuine, practical value, especially for team leaders. When assigning work, senior attorneys should strive to match projects with the team members' goals wherever possible, a boost for engagement and productivity.

Second, the exercise helps remind us that we must not fall into the trap of mapping our own motivations onto others. For example, nonlawyers may think that all lawyers are motivated by a desire for justice, but not all lawyers would name that as their number one motivation in life. Nor would it be appropriate to assume that all lawyers at white-shoe firms are motivated by compensation or competition. Everyone has different motivations, and this variety is present in all corners of our industry.

Third, the exercise promotes psychological safety by rewarding vulnerability. As discussed in Chapter 1, you cannot have psychological safety without vulnerability. Since this exercise requires sharing something personal, it forces every team member to participate at an authentic level. In fact, I encourage the most senior team members to go first, ideally the most senior partner, serving as a model for others to follow.

Finally, although the prompt pushes people outside their comfort zone, it is not a boundless invasion of their privacy. People are usually more open to discussing childhood experiences, since they happened so long ago, rather than, for example, asking attorneys to name their most embarrassing work experience from the past few years. I remind people that they do not have to share their deepest, darkest secrets. I only ask that they share something *real*.

For example, I have seen attorneys share stories about:

- Becoming a first-generation lawyer, and the parental pressure that came with that achievement
- Being a soccer player and ultimately pivoting that competitive spirit (and work ethic) into a different sort of competition via the courtroom
- Barely graduating from high school due to a battle with cancer, then winning that fight and going on to pursue an Ivy League education

Not every story shared will be worthy of a Daytime Emmy. But you will undoubtedly see your colleagues in a more human, more authentic way after an exercise like this. I cannot tell you how many lawyers, from the most transactional of transactional attorneys to battle-hardened litigators, told me that this exercise helped them get to know their team members on a deeper level despite having already worked together for years—in some cases more than a decade. And it takes as little as fifteen minutes. Talk about ROI.

EXERCISE #4: PERSONALITY ASSESSMENTS

Just as the motivation-sharing exercise provides an authentic, vulnerable experience that increases trust between team members, sharing personality assessments can have a similar effect. For example, have your team members take the formal Social Styles assessment (which you can purchase online from TRACOM) or license another assessment for your team, like DiSC, the Enneagram, or the Myers-Briggs Type Indicator, if you prefer. I have no affiliation with any of these licensors. There are pros and cons to each, but in my view, all of them provide valuable fodder for building team trust.

After all team members complete and review their assessments, have everyone share the aspects of their profile that resonate most with them. You can even open the discussion up to the group for reactions after each profile is read, encouraging them to share candid observations and feedback. But remind everyone that there are no optimal or suboptimal profiles; the exercise is designed to help get to know team members better, without judgment. These discussions tend to be incredibly illuminating.

MODELING TRUST THROUGH VULNERABILITY

Although we have discussed many concrete trust-building activities, it is worth emphasizing that sometimes, the most concrete thing a leader can do to build trust with team members is simply to model what "good trust" looks like by demonstrating vulnerability. Give a little, get a little.

A few real-world examples:

- After a deal closed, a partner conducted a "retrospective" to review what went well and what didn't. (We'll discuss retros more in Chapter 14.) He opened by admitting that he shouldn't have been so quick to reject the team's concerns about the proposed process for calculating the value of securities that investors would receive. The mechanics of the calculation, he admitted, ended up being more burdensome than he expected, all of which could have been avoided if he had been more open to the team's feedback.

- A senior associate came to a team meeting with two junior associates and opened by saying, "You should all know that I have a personal matter that's distracting me today. It's nothing too serious—a conflict with my mother that is weighing on me. But if I seem not myself today, please know that it has nothing to do with you."

- A senior partner, in reacting to a negative post on Glassdoor (a website where participants can share reviews, good or bad, about their employers), admitted to the practice group, "This one took me by surprise, and that is the thing that bothers me most. I should have had a better pulse on the team. We're going to fix this."

If these examples seem a bit too "micro," perhaps it would help to know that each of these stories was relayed to me by junior associates in response to asking for the "most meaningful examples of outstanding leadership" they witnessed from more senior attorneys. These seemingly small acts of honesty and vulnerability were so memorable that they stuck with those junior attorneys for a long time—for years, in some cases—and helped shape their vision of positive leadership.

This is yet another reminder that attorneys are not inspired by robots or demigods; they value authenticity in their leaders. If you model these values, you will inspire others to do the same.

———

When it comes to trust, the stakes are high. Without it, teams lack the psychological safety they need to take risks and be authentic in every interaction. Instead, they focus only on self-protection. They do not admit mistakes or ask for help; such actions might suggest weakness. And worse yet, their distrust prevents them from assuming colleagues have good intentions, making it more likely that a small disagreement will flare into a toxic conflict.

This is why attorneys have to take trust seriously. They have to look beyond vague buzzwords and cliches and recognize that trust is a vital ingredient for collaboration, one that lays the foundation for high performance across the board. And with so much to gain, attorneys should not wait and hope that trust forms naturally, either through the lowered inhibitions of happy hours or the high pressure of intense client work. Those who embrace a more systematic approach not only achieve results faster, but they forge stronger, more meaningful bonds on their teams.

In fact, we have only scratched the surface of these rewards. That is because trust, while beneficial in itself, is foundational. It unlocks everything else that keeps the high-performing team running at full throttle. If we can foster psychological safety on our teams—where colleagues feel comfortable being themselves, asking questions, and taking risks—we can create a trusting environment where attorneys are willing to look beyond their own needs and instead invest in the greater good of the team, the client, and the organization.

In other words, we are now ready to move to other dimensions of high-performing teams, starting with building a culture of *ownership*. But as we'll soon see, an ownership mentality does not always come naturally. Like the other key traits of high-performance legal teams, we will need to break a number of common bad habits along the way.

PART 2

OWNERSHIP

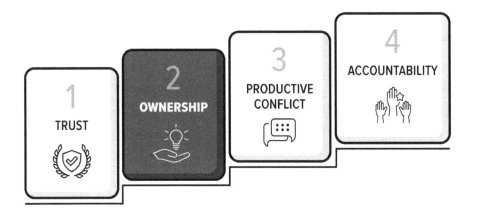

CHAPTER 5

THE BROKEN VENN DIAGRAM

Lawyers—like any other working professional—are going to have their fair share of complaints from time to time, especially in big firms. Anyone working within a large organization, with so many people and so many moving parts, is bound to run into problems, and it is not hard to pick out someone—perhaps multiple someones—responsible. Expressing these frustrations is cathartic, and so, on particularly tough days, attorneys might find themselves making a call or popping into the office of a friendly colleague with a cup of coffee to share what's on their mind.

But when the venting is done and the coffee consumed, has anything really changed? Are the problems that vexed us solved? Or have we simply found a new way to bond with team members by rallying against our common enemies?

In the last section, we learned to avoid leaping to judge colleagues' character or competency whenever a problem arises. But in this section, our high-performance legal teams confront a new threat: a breakdown in *ownership* that occurs when attorneys do not believe they have the power to solve a problem that someone else has created. This powerlessness is learned, and now, it must be unlearned.

Complaints between colleagues are perfect fodder for this conversation because they serve as manifestations of this powerlessness in action and give us ample opportunities to reset this mentality. In fact, the next two chapters in this section on ownership will be structured around lists of common concerns attorneys often have. By turning each concern into a concrete action, we will uncover an entirely new way of thinking about our role in solving the problems that plague our teams.

First, we need to explain what an "ownership mentality" really means, and why it is so important for high-performance legal teams. That will be the focus of this chapter. Then in Chapters 6 and 7, we will apply that new mentality from two different perspectives: first through the lens of a more junior attorney (seizing opportunities to manage "up") and then from a more senior attorney (managing "down"). These deep dives will help build muscle memory to break the old ways of thinking and restore a sense of ownership. Finally, Chapter 8 will explore broader best practices—and pitfalls to avoid—when creating a culture of ownership across legal teams.

DEFINING OWNERSHIP

An ownership mentality reflects a deeper, genuine commitment to the goals of the team, client, and organization, such that one works to address any roadblocks regardless of who is responsible.

While this may sound simple in theory, the execution of this mentality can be downright cryptic in practice. In fact, of the four key traits of high-performance legal teams—trust, ownership, productive conflict, and accountability—ownership can be the most difficult to internalize, especially in the initial stages of an attorney's career.

I'll give an example. Early in my own career, I recall a partner sitting down to review some of our team's work and telling us, "You need to own the whole case." I found this advice bewildering at the time. We were working long hours. Was he doubting our commitment? Didn't he know we were all new to this and trying our best? You may have heard similarly ambiguous advice pop up in your career in different forms. Some attorneys might be told, "You need to think like a partner." Or, "You have to take more initiative." In the business world, one might hear, "You need to think like a CEO."

What does any of that really mean? Unfortunately, many people do not unlock this puzzling advice until they actually reach partner or some executive-equivalent role, far too late for the suggestion to help them. As we will see, despite the different phrasing, these statements are actually conveying the same message.

Let's demystify this concept by starting small. Imagine you are an attorney at a firm of one: a sole proprietorship. You have no associates. No paralegals or assistants. It's just you against the world.

Now imagine you are working on a matter for one of your clients when you encounter a problem: the internet goes out. What do you do? Call the IT team? Oh, right—they don't exist. So now you have to spend valuable time on the phone with your internet service provider trying to troubleshoot the problem. The internet is not going to fix itself, after all.

When you run your own business, you are acutely aware that every problem is your problem to solve. Power goes out? Look for the circuit breaker. Not getting enough clients? Time to learn digital marketing. Having trouble filing that motion? Better call the clerk's office—and fast.

As you grow your business, you happily expand your team, and increasingly you are able to delegate responsibility to others. But if it is still *your* business, then at the end of the day, no matter what the roadblock is, *you* have to figure it out. The fact that someone else on your team *could* or *should* be able to handle this roadblock might be comforting, but if that person falls down on the job, you have to be ready to step in and solve the problem.

A CEO from one of my trainings put it this way:

> Before I became CEO, I looked up to other CEOs and was intimidated by their ability to address any challenge in the business. I thought to myself, "I could never do that." Then I became a CEO myself and realized that they didn't have all the answers. No CEO does. We just don't have any choice but to try. If we don't, no one else will.

That's ownership. It doesn't matter what the CEO's job description actually says. The CEO's job is to solve the biggest problems facing the business—full stop. They can leverage their team or their network—or do it themselves—but either way, CEOs do not just sit around complaining about a problem; *they take action.* (Or they do not stay in the job very long.)

By contrast, few employees feel this same sense of ownership, especially when they are just one person in a large organization.

Complaining about a problem, rather than doing something about it, is a typical fallback position. That gap is what we want to address.

Even though most attorneys do not run their own businesses or law firms, they can still possess an ownership mentality. In fact, no matter how junior you are in your organization, taking ownership can allow you to extend your influence far beyond your job description. And in fact, this mentality can catapult your career.

But this raises questions. Can one really be expected to address every problem? Isn't that unrealistic? And don't we want attorneys to stay focused on their work, not delve into other people's problems?

These are all reasonable questions. To answer them, we have to stop talking about the theory of ownership and instead talk about ownership in practice.

COMMON CONCERNS

If ownership is about addressing problems, we need some problems to solve. We will begin with a list of common concerns that attorneys have about their bosses from time to time. As you read this list, consider whether you have ever had one of these complaints about your manager:

1. *My manager is disorganized.*
2. *My manager does not give clear direction.*
3. *My manager does not give me helpful feedback.*
4. *My manager does not care about my career.*
5. *My manager is never available when needed.*
6. *My manager micromanages me.*

A few of these are probably familiar. Everyone has had moments of frustration with a boss at some point in their career. Even partners occasionally feel frustrated with their own bosses (more senior partners and firm leaders). But complaints are not a one-way street. Just as more junior attorneys may have concerns about their managers, managers often have trouble with team members they oversee. Managers' concerns might include the following:

1. *I never get what I asked for from this team member.*
2. *They come to me with problems, not solutions.*
3. *I always have to bug them for status updates.*
4. *They get stuck on things that don't matter.*
5. *They don't keep track of the big picture.*

Now comes the big question: who is responsible for fixing these problems?

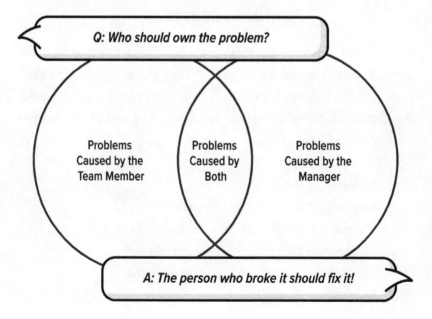

Most people think of responsibility a bit like a Venn diagram—two overlapping circles. There are problems caused by the more junior team member in the circle on the left, and problems caused by the manager on the right. Sometimes, both are responsible for the issue, so we have that intersection in the middle. We would then expect whoever created the problem to fix it, right?

This conclusion is tempting—and intuitive—but also *dead wrong*. Feel free to get out a pen and draw a giant "X" right over that image. Erase this broken Venn diagram from your mind. It is a false idol.

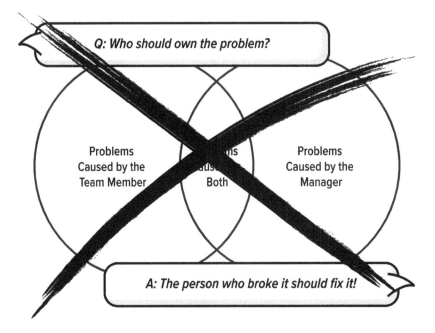

A true ownership mentality sets blame aside. If the person who caused the issue is not stepping up, after all, the problem is still a problem. So who is going to fix it? The answer is unavoidable: you are.

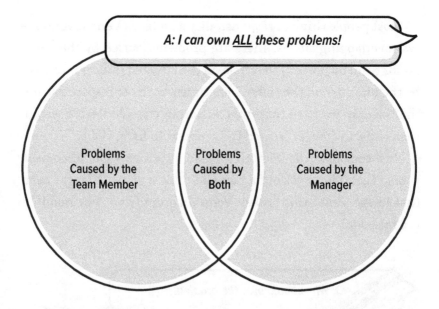

This is the path of ownership. Of course, it is not the only path. When faced with a problem on your team, you have several options:

1. You could accept the problem as a fact of life (and take no action).
2. You could leave the team or organization.
3. You could give feedback to those better positioned to fix the problem.
4. You could take direct action yourself to steer the solution.

Attorneys often do not think #4 is a realistic option because, from their vantage point, they do not see any meaningful, constructive action they could take. That is the thinking I want to challenge. Over the next two chapters, we are going to take these lists of concerns and show how to apply an ownership mentality to address each problem. In doing so, this concept will come into sharper focus.

As you will see, although ownership does have practical limits—meaning, you cannot realistically solve *every* problem or change *every* mind—you can *contribute* in a meaningful way. Any complaint can be turned into *action*. And as you adopt this mentality, you may come to realize you are capable of far more than you thought. Once the entire team adopts this mentality, the sky's the limit.

CHAPTER 6

MANAGING UP

n my seminars on ownership, attorneys with concerns about their managers routinely explain they have not taken ownership of those issues because they lack the power to do anything useful. As a lowly junior attorney, for example, how could you coax the managing attorney to run better meetings, conduct career growth conversations, or stop micromanaging the team?

In this chapter, we will debunk the myth that a person needs title and authority to get things done. Take CEOs, for instance. Despite extensive decision-making authority over strategy, budget, and hiring or firing that should theoretically let them snap their fingers and bend companies to their will, CEOs will tell you that their omnipotence is a myth. Rarely can a CEO make a significant decision without consulting others and winning their support. This commitment to collaboration is how they *earn* their influence, a source of power that has little to do with their title and everything to do with their leadership style.

Indeed, having to "order" someone to do something—over the person's objections—is the *last* resort for strong leaders, who recognize that such forceful actions reduce their credibility, destroy morale, and weaken the team as a whole.

So too must junior team members recognize that their position in the hierarchy is not a ceiling on their power. That is not to say their power is unlimited; it is not. But most attorneys far underestimate their capacity to influence the team around them.

In the last chapter, we identified six common concerns attorneys might have about their managers. Now, we will work through each scenario and apply an ownership mentality, finding concrete ways to take action that could improve the situation—all without challenging the manager's higher title and authority. At first, this task may seem daunting. But with repetition, several common themes will emerge.

A few hints before we get started. An ownership mentality starts by *setting aside blame*. Instead, we turn that attention inward, asking, "What can I do to fix the situation, regardless of who caused the problem?" Next, we have to *define the problem*. This sometimes means peeling back layers of the problem like an onion to expose different ways to think about (and eventually address) the situation. Finally, in the solution stage, we brainstorm *concrete actions* we can take that might help address the problem. We may not be able to snap our fingers and make every problem disappear, but any meaningful improvement we achieve will translate directly into a better experience for us and our team members.

The goal here is for this approach to become second nature. If you can own these six problems, turning each concern into concrete action, then you can extend that thinking to virtually any problem in your workplace. For each scenario below, imagine you are the attorney voicing this complaint and consider how you might own the problem yourself.

SCENARIO #1: "MY MANAGER IS DISORGANIZED."

If you read this prompt and immediately wanted to know what specific *behavior* the manager actually committed to trigger this accusation, you passed the first test. Disorganization can manifest in many ways on a team, so before you can own this problem—or any problem—you have to define the problem more carefully. As currently worded, this complaint is vague and unconstructive. Calling the manager "disorganized" implies some innate character trait, which suggests we are being influenced by the fundamental attribution error or differences in working styles (or both).

So let's get more specific: imagine that the manager's team meetings are the cause for concern. There are no agendas, and the manager often meanders from topic to topic and back again. Half the meeting might end up being devoted to an issue specific to only one associate, wasting everyone else's time. And at the end, the action items are unclear, leading to confusion and—adding insult to injury—more meetings.

If you are "just another team member" in the group, not a manager yourself, what could you do to address this problem?

First, you might share constructive feedback with the manager. This can be a tricky conversation, which is why there is an entire chapter dedicated to feedback later in this book. If you genuinely care about solving the problem, then taking time to plan and deliver thoughtful feedback is time well spent. In fact, feedback is a good option in just about every scenario we will discuss related to ownership because each of our scenarios involves someone else's actions. Feedback is a critical mechanism for helping others improve their behavior so that they can grow.

But feedback is not the only path here. Even if you provide great feedback, it might not solve the problem. After all, feedback still implies that the problem—disorganized meetings—is the manager's problem to solve. Although that is 100% true—the manager can and should run better meetings—the goal of this chapter is to go further and brainstorm additional solutions. So for the purposes of this exercise, consider how *you* can solve the problem even if the manager apparently cannot.

Think about the problem this way: is there a rule that says only a manager can organize a team meeting?

I used to think so. On my very first day of my very first case at Boston Consulting Group, the project leader—their equivalent of a mid-level associate—sat me down and told me that one of my jobs on the team was to assemble the agenda for our team meetings. I asked how I—a junior consultant who did not even understand yet what the case was *about*—could possibly know what is most important for the team to discuss. He explained:

> Obviously, you don't. So how would you find out? Each week, you'll connect with every team member and ask them what issues they need to discuss. Make a list of those issues and rank them based on your best guess as to their importance. Then I'll review your list and make changes or reorder if needed.

He also warned me not to be a scribe: "Don't just mindlessly write down what another team member tells you. I'm going to expect you to be able to explain each issue to me, so ask follow-up questions if you don't understand."

That seemingly innocuous administrative task forced me to get up to speed quickly on the case and understand what my colleagues were doing. The additional responsibility offered me a development opportunity, and it freed up the manager's time. Not surprisingly, that project leader, with his knack for marshaling resources, had little trouble making partner a few years later.

In my example, the manager was the one who had this idea, but junior team members can easily flip the script. By making an unsolicited offer to take on organizational duties for the team, a team member can effectively fill in the gap left by a manager. If concerned about stepping on toes, keep the wording nonjudgmental. For example, a more junior attorney might say to the manager:

> I noticed we have a lot to cover in team meetings. Would it help if I coordinate with the other associates and provide a list of topics we'd propose discussing? You can then review the draft and add or change it up as needed. I'm also happy to take notes in the meeting and circulate a list of any action items we agree on.

Few managers would say no to this offer.

It's true that this path likely means a bit more work for *you*, the junior team member. But ownership means rolling up one's sleeves to help fill gaps regardless of who is to blame. Besides, solving the problem by ensuring more effective meetings will ultimately *save* you and the entire team time in the future.

SCENARIO #2: "MY MANAGER DOES NOT GIVE CLEAR DIRECTION."

Nearly every attorney has shared this experience: a more senior attorney calls you and asks for assistance with something. After explaining the task, you wisely ask, "When do you need this done by?"

The response: "No set deadline, but sooner is better."

Vague answers like this one can be particularly vexing to junior associates who lack sufficient context to know how to prioritize new tasks handed to them on a whim. But ambiguous instructions happen, and they are not limited to deadlines. For example, an attorney may be handed an open-ended research question, and after a dozen hours compiling a ten-page memo, find out that the senior attorney only wanted a few bullet points from one jurisdiction. Or a partner, in response to a senior leader's question about the practice group's "long-term strategy," sends a simple email with a few thoughts, only to be told a more extensive presentation was expected, backed by budget projections.

If you are handed an ambiguous task, what can you do to solve the problem? Start by defining the problem blamelessly. Usually, the underlying issue is that the manager does not realize that the instruction could have more than one interpretation. Someone giving you an assignment may simply think—incorrectly—that there is only one, self-evident interpretation.

Next, you could try to solve the problem by explaining to the manager the various interpretations you have in mind. Doing so will invite the manager to clarify. For example:

PROBLEM TO OWN	POTENTIAL APPROACH
Ambiguous deadline	Give a somewhat extreme range to trigger the manager to clarify. E.g., "Are you thinking this will take me closer to an hour—or a week?"
Ambiguous research scope	Conduct a thirty- to sixty-minute "speed run" with the goal—*not* of completing the task—but of learning *just enough* to estimate how long it will take to complete. Then share your estimate with your manager along with your proposed scope, and ask if this sounds like the right direction.
Ambiguous presentation format	Request examples of prior presentations. If none exists, draft a rough template in your medium of choice and ask if, once filled in, such a presentation would align with expectations.

These are all examples of encouraging parameters without being "pushy." If we were to instead say to the manager, "Please be more specific," or, "I don't understand what you want," the manager still might not understand *what* is confusing. By being more concrete, we help the manager spot the ambiguity—and correct it.

SCENARIO #3: "MY MANAGER DOES NOT GIVE ME HELPFUL FEEDBACK."

When I was a junior associate, I remember being disappointed by my first review. The problem was not that I received tough feedback; the problem was that I received *too little* tough feedback. This is not a "humble brag." Many attorneys have had a similar experience of receiving well-intentioned, positive reviews that stroke the ego but fail to deliver actionable feedback that can aid in their development. We all want to improve, but sometimes, concrete feedback simply does not come.

Now consider how an ownership mentality can unlock better feedback from one's manager. Again, start by defining the problem without judgment. Why might an attorney be uncomfortable or unwilling to give constructive feedback?

One of the biggest challenges people have in giving feedback is a lack of psychological safety. Many managers have feedback to offer but worry that sharing it will damage the relationship, especially if they are conflict-averse. In essence, many managers ironically worry that their junior team members will judge *them* for how they deliver feedback. Without a culture of candid feedback, they opt for the safer path of ego-stroking and sugarcoating.

Framed this way, the "problem to solve" is how to make it easier for your manager to give feedback. The solution could include making it clear you want the feedback, giving the manager proper time to prepare, and accepting feedback without being defensive.

For example, you are unlikely to get rich, candid feedback if you pop by unannounced and ask for ways to improve—or worse, when you slip a question about feedback in between the appetizer and main course at a team dinner. Rather than catching the manager off guard, you might instead send an email explaining your intentions. E.g., "Now that the deal is closed, I'd like to get your feedback. I scheduled thirty minutes on your calendar Tuesday. Feel free to push it back if you need more time." You can even offer a feedback agenda—a list of two or three specific topics you'd like covered—to soften the ground.

We will cover more detailed tips for soliciting feedback in Chapter 16. But hopefully you can already see how these seemingly small actions might have a meaningful impact. If you instead just write the manager off as being "bad at feedback," the situation is unlikely to change.

SCENARIO #4: "MY MANAGER DOES
NOT CARE ABOUT MY CAREER."

In Chapter 3, we discussed the conflict between Greg and Lisa, two associates who failed to get along largely because of severe clashes in their working styles. One of Lisa's complaints about Greg was his myopic focus on the next urgent task, never taking time for bigger picture conversations about Lisa's career or development. She felt this was because Greg simply "didn't care." In fact, Greg did care—he privately shared with me his regret at not mentoring his team members better—but struggled with the more extreme instincts of his driver Social Style; for him, maintaining control of tasks and timelines was the most important priority, and he never had time left for investing in others' career development.

If Lisa had known this, what could she have done to solve the problem, despite the fact that she was not the one who *caused* the problem?

Instead of hoping Greg would intersperse career development conversations naturally during their one-on-one sessions, Lisa could have instead recognized that she needed a more structured approach for someone as task-driven as Greg. For example, following the same vein as Scenario #3, Lisa could have scheduled time in advance with Greg for a career development conversation and set an agenda for what she wanted to cover. Drivers appreciate agendas, after all, and Lisa could have booked the session during a relatively quiet week to reduce the risk that Greg would be distracted.

An attorney in this situation could also try framing the conversation around "seeking advice" from the more experienced attorney. Most people find this request flattering and are happy to share guidance when asked direct questions. Even basic questions like, "What do you wish you had known earlier in your career?" can be a nearly universal conversation starter for career advice. And by inviting advice, you might just turn the manager into your supporter, and in time, a genuine advocate.

None of this means Greg is "off the hook" for his management shortfalls—a concern we will address more directly in Chapter 8. We are simply exploring pragmatic solutions that might yield progress regardless of who is at fault.

SCENARIO #5: "MY MANAGER IS NEVER AVAILABLE WHEN NEEDED."

Our fifth scenario involves a problem with a manager whose schedule is packed so tightly that the attorney is often unavailable, even when needed most. An overloaded manager can generate all sorts of friction on a team, through inconveniently scheduled meetings, late nights fueled by last-minute emails, or a lack of guidance altogether.

Hopefully, you have picked up on patterns from the previous scenarios and have already started to reframe this problem more constructively. Instead of an "unavailable manager," you might think of this instead as a "planning and scheduling challenge"—tricky, but hardly insurmountable.

Although you are not technically responsible for your manager's calendar, you are nevertheless capable of brainstorming strategies to mitigate the problem. For example, you might schedule time in advance—before it's needed—such as setting check-in calls to occur the day before every deadline, anticipating that you will probably need that time for last-minute issues. If done a week in advance, it will be easier to block that time. Or, when seeking advice, you might write emails that lay out two to three specific options the manager can choose from, making it easier to respond with a simple "go with #2," instead of having to write a lengthy response to your open-ended question. Finally, to avoid a whirlwind of last-minute feedback on your work product before the deadline, you might send the manager an outline early on in the timeline, allowing you to confirm you are heading in the right direction, rather than waiting until a draft is mostly complete to seek feedback.

It's true that the manager could—and should—think of these same actions, rather than a more junior team member having to step into those shoes. But even if the manager falls short, any team member has the power to take ownership of—and fix—the problem.

SCENARIO #6: "MY MANAGER MICROMANAGES ME."

The final example is one of the most challenging. In Chapter 2, we discussed how the fundamental attribution error might lead us to write off a micromanaging attorney as a "bad manager" and leave it at that. We learned to overcome this barrier by considering what *positive intentions* might underlie this behavior so that we might approach the situation with an open mind.

But aside from opening an avenue of feedback, we did not explore other concrete solutions an attorney might employ to break the micromanagement cycle. To apply an ownership mentality here, we will need to identify and address the problem driving the micromanager's behavior.

Put yourself in the shoes of a micromanager overseeing multiple workstreams. Because micromanagers care deeply about the work being "done right," their biggest fear is allowing poor quality work to slip past their defenses. And with so many work-streams to oversee, the manager may have difficulty keeping track of what each person is doing. This lack of visibility—and lack of control—is the fear that is driving the behavior. Simply put, the micromanager does not trust the team member to get the job done right. The question then becomes how to *earn* that manager's trust.

Now imagine that one attorney on the team goes above and beyond to communicate plans and progress to the manager. When assigned a project, this attorney emails the manager within a few hours confirming the scope and deadline of the project and even lays out a rough plan of attack. The attorney maintains a shared spreadsheet listing current tasks and updates it once a week with the status so the manager can follow the progress. And when delivering work product, the attorney explicitly notes any stones left "unturned" (e.g., legal theories left unexplored because they seem too tenuous), so that the manager can confirm such paths are indeed unnecessary.

In other words, this attorney does the same legal work as any other attorney, but *communicates* about the work more precisely and proactively than anyone else.

For a micromanager, such clear communication is like a warm blanket on a snowy day. If there are problems, they can be corrected early to keep the project on track. If the attorney needs more time, the manager will learn about it before the deadline, not after it has already passed. And the sheer level of organization demonstrated by the attorney's communication makes clear that this attorney is unlikely to let things fall through the cracks. Slowly but steadily, the micromanager trusts that this person has things under control and shifts attention to less disciplined team members.

Some might worry that more communication might *invite* micromanagement. In fact, some attorneys, in an effort to keep a micromanager away, will avoid CC'ing the micromanager on emails, provide only terse updates, and push back on any requests they feel invade their autonomy.

Bad idea. This kind of passive-aggressive behavior does not imbue trust; it destroys it. The only way to get a micromanager to be more hands-off is to earn the person's trust, and pushing the manager away affords no such opportunity. While it is entirely reasonable to be frustrated that the micromanager's bar for trust is so high—after all, you are an intelligent, hard-working attorney who should be trusted to do good work—simply refusing to engage the manager will not magically bring that bar down any lower. It will only bring tensions to a boil.

Moreover, proactive communication is a best practice even when working for healthy, trusting managers. Many attorneys simply do not communicate in this way because they think it takes up too much time and has too few benefits. But consider this simple email template attorneys could use to send a weekly update to managers about their work:

Hi [manager],

Below is my weekly update for my workstream. Let me know if you have any questions.

- Progress made this week: ...

- Plans for next week: ...

- Potential roadblocks: ...

- Key things I may need from you next week: ...

Thanks,
[Name]

This may seem pedantic, but this kind of email takes *five minutes* to write before closing shop each Friday, and the impact can be substantial. For those of you who are managers, you can probably appreciate why: proactive communication like this suggests the attorney is reliable and organized. When you have a large team to manage, you will focus your efforts on the weakest links. By contrast, the team member who sends emails like these would be your golden child.

———

Throughout your career, you will work with people who have flaws. Even your managers, despite perhaps having more training, experience, and expertise than you, will make missteps that drive you up the wall from time to time. But a true ownership mentality frees you from playing the blame game and instead positions you to be a problem solver rather than simply a problem spotter.

Another limitation of the blame game is that it tends to result in the blame going everywhere—except yourself. The truth is, for every problem we have at work, we are likely contributing to that problem at least in some small way, either through our actions or

perhaps our inaction. The ownership mentality sets aside judgment. There is no weighing of fault. The only path forward is to
focus on what *you* can do to help set things on course.

Hopefully, the six scenarios we reviewed help demonstrate
how ownership works in practice, not just in theory, allowing us
to attack problems that previously might have seemed beyond
our control. In a nutshell, our framework has three steps.

OWNERSHIP IN ACTION

1. **Set aside blame.** When you feel a complaint boiling to the
   surface, turn that frustration into something constructive by
   attacking the *problem*, not the *person*.
2. **Define the problem carefully.** Peel back the layers of the
   problem without letting the fundamental attribution error or
   differences in working styles color your objectivity.
3. **Brainstorm concrete actions.** Inaction is the only sure path
   to failure. If you are willing to take action, even if you only
   move the needle a little bit at a time, you will gain momentum
   toward your larger goals.

Admittedly, this mentality can be exhausting. Fixing problems
caused by others can be frustrating at best and downright depress-
ing at worst. In Chapter 8, we will talk about how to draw healthy
boundaries. But more often than not, attorneys who are willing
to set aside blame and focus on solving problems will be happier
and more successful than those who fall back into an understandable—but ultimately unproductive—spiral of manager-bashing.

By all means, if you have legitimate concerns, you should share them constructively with your manager and other leaders (including HR representatives). They are there to help. But if you are simply complaining to a colleague over coffee, just keep in mind that while the conversation may feel cathartic, the buzz will be short-lived.

To be clear, I am not telling junior team members that they—and not their leaders—bear the responsibility of ensuring their teams are managed effectively. This is not about shifting responsibility; this is about *collective* responsibility. As we will see, ownership works best when it works both ways. While it is ultimately the manager's responsibility to manage well, junior team members can contribute too, helping the whole team rise in the process. In the next chapter, it will be the managers' turn to exercise this mindset.

CHAPTER 7

MANAGING DOWN

"Is it me, or is it them?"

At some point, virtually every attorney who manages a team will ask this question. Even the most optimistic attorney can become exasperated with a team member, especially if that is the *only* team member who just doesn't seem to "get it." If the manager has been consistent with the same instructions and guidance across the board, but one team member simply does not perform like the others, it's understandable to wonder, "Aren't they the problem?"

When managers think this way, I cannot help but think of the image on the previous page.

When you are a manager, you never have the option to write off a challenge as "their" problem. Every problem on your team is, ultimately, *your* problem to own. After all, despite the captain's flippant attitude, he (and his ship) are going down. Maybe your instructions and management style seem to work for most other team members, but this is not an excuse to throw up your hands in the face of an outlier. In fact, these situations can teach us the most about management, because they remind us that everyone is different.

For managers, an ownership mentality means a *teaching* mentality. Throughout this chapter, we will explore scenarios that put this idea to the test, even in the face of seemingly "unteachable" skill gaps. This is difficult terrain. After all, teaching is a discipline in itself; people go to school for years just to learn the core principles, after which they spend more years perfecting their craft. This chapter will not adequately do justice to that experience. But at a minimum, we can identify (and break) a number of managing attorneys' bad habits and build a set of concrete tactics that can address common challenges.

In each of the five scenarios below, we have a team member—or multiple team members—whose behavior is a pain point for the manager. Put yourself in the position of the managing attorney and think about what you might do to own the problem. Start by setting judgment aside; then define the problem carefully; and finally, brainstorm practical steps you could take to improve the situation. Along the way, you may start to notice common themes.

SCENARIO #1: "I NEVER GET WHAT I ASKED FOR FROM THIS TEAM MEMBER."

In one of my coaching sessions, a senior associate from a large law firm expressed frustration about a team member who turned in an assignment with only three of the five tasks done on a deal she was overseeing. While she could understand a junior associate making mistakes in executing a task, she asked me what could possibly explain the person turning in an assignment with two of the tasks missing entirely?

Her exasperation was understandable, but she was making a common mistake, one we have already seen several times in this book. She was asking the *right* question, but to the wrong person. Rhetorical questions—such as, "How could they possibly...?" and "Why would they do that?"—are simply judgments masked as interrogatories. They are meant to imply that there is no reasonable explanation for the team member's behavior, and that the only conclusion is that the person simply lacks the necessary capability or commitment. But this attitude undermines trust and flies in the face of psychological safety. To truly own the problem, the manager has to start by turning these rhetorical questions into genuine ones.

If you are the manager in this situation, you can start by opening a dialogue with the junior associate and ask about the missing tasks—ideally in person or over the phone to avoid appearing passive-aggressive in an email or text chat. Doing so might allow new facts to come to light. For example, it is quite common for a manager to *think* the instructions about an assignment were clear, but the junior associate nevertheless interpreted the conversation differently. When asked why certain tasks were overlooked, the junior associate, with a quizzical look, might respond simply, "I didn't know you wanted me to do that."

Instead of letting irritation take over, an ownership mentality requires you as the manager to avoid judging the associate and instead identify ways you could help reduce miscommunications in the future.

For example, after an oral conversation about a new assignment, you might ask the associate to email a quick recap of the task "just to confirm we are on the same page." The simple act of writing down action items often reveals when those items were inherently unclear, allowing ambiguity to be nipped in the bud. Ultimately, by ensuring expectations are aligned and in writing, both you and the team member will benefit.

Once we pivot from judgment to problem-solving, this scenario becomes straightforward. Next, let's look at a more challenging concern.

SCENARIO #2: "THEY ALWAYS COME TO ME WITH PROBLEMS, NOT SOLUTIONS."

When an attorney hits a roadblock, it is common—even appropriate—for them to ping the manager for help. But when taken too far, this Q&A morphs into a cycle of enablement: knowing that the manager is always available to troubleshoot problems, attorneys may not build the self-confidence they need to address challenges on their own. Associates simply delegate all higher-level thinking "up" to the manager. The manager then gets used to being in the weeds on every issue. As a result, associates can end up unwittingly contributing to their own micromanagement.

For example, imagine a litigation associate who asks the partner for help reaching a witness who has not responded to emails in several days. Chances are, the partner does not have a secret phone number for the witness or some kind of bat light that can bring forth the witness from the shadows. In fact, the partner has roughly the same options as the associate—another email or phone call—albeit with the added weight of the partner's name behind it. While good managers are happy to help, managers who always snap their fingers to solve team members' problems can actually impede growth.

So if you were the partner in this scenario, instead of jumping in to save the day, you could turn this into a teaching opportunity. You can ask the litigation associate to recommend two to three options with the associate's highest recommendation first. Then discuss. Once the associate zeroes in on the right answer— perhaps with a bit of nudging—you can authorize the associate to take action (emphasizing that the associate is still in charge of the witness relationship).

This situation may seem basic, but the framework applies to more complex legal roadblocks as well. For example, imagine a corporate client seeking guidance on whether a business initiative runs afoul of new securities regulations, and the associate assigned the task is having trouble finding authority one way or another to resolve the question. The partner, with many years of experience advising clients through such ambiguities, might have a sense of the best course of action to recommend to the client. But rather than hand this wisdom to the associate on a silver platter, the partner could ask the associate for a few options, the pros and cons of each, and the potential risks, leaning on the associate to drive the discussion. Of course, the partner will have the final say. But the conversation will, as the saying goes, teach the associate how to fish.

This is empowerment in action—a topic we will discuss more in the next chapter. It does not mean granting unlimited authority; it simply means demonstrating that you, as the manager, believe the more junior attorney has the skill and wisdom to find the solution. Nor does this mean giving up control; you can still retain approval authority and make that clear to them. But by asking team members to propose solutions, you are encouraging them to have an ownership mentality themselves. That is how ownership proliferates.

SCENARIO #3: "I ALWAYS HAVE TO BUG THEM FOR STATUS UPDATES."

Radio silence can induce anxiety for many managers. Sitting at a desk, unsure of the team's progress, watching the clock wind down until deliverables are due—a manager could be forgiven for frayed nerves. Will everything come together at the last minute? Will the work product be up to par? Or will it be a long night ahead fixing problems and filling gaps before the deadline?

But team members are usually unaware of these managerial concerns. In fact, they believe that by going "heads down" and not surfacing until the work is done, they are displaying their independence and autonomy, traits that are typically admirable. They do not understand that more proactive communication along the way actually benefits them by giving the manager an opportunity to catch problems or misunderstandings about an assignment early, reducing rework and last-minute scrambling.

For junior team members, there is a valuable insight in here about distinguishing yourself through better communication. But for managers, the broader point is that it is unfair to "expect" junior team members to be more proactive in communication unless you have made those expectations clear. If you want better communication, create space for it.

For example, too often, managing attorneys assign a complex task and give only a single deadline—nothing more. Armed with that one deadline, the team member has no reason to come up for air until the assignment is complete (or a significant problem arises). Instead, managers could specifically propose interim milestones, such as dates when an outline or draft is due, or schedule a check-in call mid-week to discuss progress. Or better yet, ask the team member to propose those milestones to ensure the process is collaborative. In Chapter 15, we will dive deeper into the delegation process to ensure we strike the right balance of management without micromanagement.

If concerned this tactic may come off pedantic, be open about that fear, remembering that vulnerability can engender trust. For example: "Team, I'd like to propose this structured timeline. I worry this may come off draconian, so let me explain why I'm doing it. And please, as I'm talking, if you have suggestions on better ways to strike a balance, jump in so we can discuss." That's the tone of a leader who wants to help the team, not control them.

SCENARIO #4: "THEY GET STUCK ON
THINGS THAT DON'T MATTER."

Attorneys learn to be thorough from the day they start law school. Issue spotting is, after all, rewarded on law school exams. What law school sometimes fails to teach, however, is *prioritization*. Students are routinely asked to spot the most issues in the shortest amount of time, not rank which issues are more important from a practical perspective. As a result, some lawyers find it difficult to ignore even the slightest loose thread. This attention to detail is laudable, but in some cases, it can be problematic. Team members, especially junior associates, can spend hours distracted by tangential legal mysteries instead of focusing more time on core issues.

Rather than metaphorically shaking a fist at the imperfections of legal education—or worse, blaming the associate for lacking prioritization as though such skills can be acquired by taking a red pill—the manager can set aside blame and instead focus on how to fill the gap. Here, the ownership mentality once again requires a *teaching* mentality. How can a manager teach a more junior attorney how to avoid getting caught in rabbit holes?

The key is to catch this behavior earlier. If the manager can step in just as the attorney is getting stuck, the manager can have a conversation with the attorney about prioritization in real time, rather than trying to reconstruct the attorney's thinking in hindsight.

With that goal in mind, we could brainstorm several possible solutions for catching rabbit-hole behavior earlier. For example:

- Halfway to the deadline, the manager could stop by the associate's office or send a message asking how the associate is doing and offering to answer any questions.
- Taking a page from the previous scenario, the manager could provide a more detailed set of checkpoints for the assignment—e.g., outline due Monday, Part I due Tuesday, and so on—allowing the manager to monitor progress more closely.
- The manager could "time-box" the assignment, e.g., "If you spend more than two hours on this question and can't find the answer, stop and check in with me."
- The manager could enact a "surface, don't solve" rule, asking team members who come across unexpected issues to surface these to the manager but not attempt to solve them until the manager gives the go-ahead. (This is particularly useful for avoiding situations where associates might stumble onto problems that have already been resolved or deemed out of scope.)

We will revisit and expand on these techniques in Chapter 15 when we dive deeper into best practices for encouraging autonomy. But the point here is that the manager has a number of options for addressing concerns about an associate getting stuck. And each of these solutions unlocks an opportunity for teaching.

SCENARIO #5: "THEY DON'T KEEP TRACK OF THE BIG PICTURE."

This final scenario tends to crop up more for senior associates, junior partners, and other attorneys on the cusp of leadership positions in their organizations. As future leaders, they must pivot from focusing on projects to focusing on *the practice* itself or on the firm more broadly—a mental shift that is harder than it sounds. For more senior partners, general counsel, or executives managing these "up-and-comers," it can be frustrating when promising attorneys seem unable to make that shift. And it can be tempting to write them off as "hitting their ceiling."

This problem—how to get an attorney to see the bigger picture—may seem difficult to "own" from the perspective of that person's manager, but that is only because its ambiguity makes the problem seem so amorphous. After all, "big picture thinking" is not a course one can simply take online. But that must not deter you.

For more ambiguous coaching challenges like this one, the trick is to make it more concrete by focusing on specific situations where you notice the problem. That is where coaching becomes possible. That is, rather than offer clichéd, generic advice like, "You have to stop missing the forest for the trees," instead, try to identify two to three specific examples where the more junior attorney made a misstep, and turn each one into a dialogue. Probe the attorney's thought process and look for the precise moment where the problem occurred. Then consider how that situation could have been avoided.

One common factor for helping attorneys see the bigger picture is whether more senior leaders take the time to share broader business context in the first place. Many years ago, I was working on a strategic initiative for a large Australian grocery chain. We were engaged in a massive in-store test that, if successful, could result in one hundred million dollars or more in additional revenue. But the in-house counsel assigned to the team called me one day to tell me that there was a problem: because the test involved some last-minute price changes on certain items, the weekly circular—those printed fliers with prices and coupons for customers—would be unavoidably out of sync with the prices in store. Thinking this hardly sounded like much of a crisis, I emailed the attorney back, asking, "Is this a low, medium, or high priority issue?"

His response: "High. Because the prices won't match, it would be false advertising. No way around it."

Frustrated, I interrogated the attorney with a series of pointed follow-up questions. By the end of our exchange, it became clear that the prices in-store would be *lower* than advertised in the circular, a benefit to shoppers that would likely not raise complaints. This would occur in two stores in the entire country, and only for a handful of items. And with that in mind, the attorney could not come up with any colorable explanation for how the company could face meaningful liability under Australian law. How could this be a "high priority" issue on a project worth nearly $100M? The attorney, in my mind, had no ability to see the bigger picture. I was ready to ask that he be replaced on this project.

That was when I realized that the actual failing was mine as the strategy leader. The attorney had been added to the team late in the game, with very little context. In an effort to minimize the burden on him, we barely included him in team conversations. Essentially, we treated the attorney like a cog in the machine, and that was how he acted. He was sent a question, and he gave an answer. He had no ability to see the bigger picture because he was never *invited* into the bigger picture.

Senior attorneys often make the same mistake, particularly at law firms. My advice: take the time to share the vision of the firm and the practice group with associates, even junior associates. Explain the strategy and how the junior associate's clients fit into that strategy. Many senior leaders mistakenly assume that more junior attorneys do not care about the practice group's or the firm's strategy, but most actually find it fascinating. They ordinarily do not get to "peek behind the curtain," and once they do, they usually feel a deeper connection to the firm. Sharing the vision with them demonstrates that you are investing in their future.

If all else fails, do not give up; ask for help. At most organizations, you are surrounded by thoughtful colleagues and supported by teams with expertise in professional development, talent management, and HR. Leverage these resources to help you become a better teacher and mentor.

It is not unusual for leaders to be frustrated with their team members from time to time. But for managers, ownership means finding ways to help team members overcome roadblocks and reach their fullest potential, which often requires slowing down to develop team members. If we skip this step—if we do not take the time to teach—we end up micromanaging by necessity and never achieve the leverage necessary for high-performance teams.

Hopefully, this chapter helped demonstrate the practical side of an ownership mentality. Using these scenarios, we identified a number of concrete tactics for owning common management challenges. Below is a summary of five key takeaways managers should bear in mind.

TACTICS FOR OWNING MANAGEMENT CHALLENGES

1. **Engage in dialogue**. Turn rhetorical questions—e.g., "Why would the associate do that?"—into genuine ones, opening a conversation to better define the root problem.

2. **Teach an attorney to fish**. For managers, an ownership mentality means a teaching mentality. Ask questions and invite them to share their thinking so that you can help guide them to the answer, not simply hand it to them.

3. **Focus on communication**. Many points of friction between managers and team members can be resolved by better communication—e.g., documenting action items, asking for interim deliverables, and checking in for questions.

4. **Get specific**. When confronted with a skills gap that seems unteachable, like wanting associates to "think big picture," pick specific examples and discuss them in-depth to surface more concrete, actionable learnings.

5. **Ask for help**. Lawyers who become managers do not suddenly transform into expert teachers and mentors. Leverage peers, senior leaders, and other in-house resources (e.g., your professional development and HR teams) as thought partners.

We spent the last two chapters turning common concerns into constructive action. For those who feel empowered by this mentality, the next question becomes: how do I get the rest of my team to adopt this same way of thinking? This can be a difficult needle to thread because, as we will see, the tools that create an environment where ownership can thrive can also be the means of its unraveling. Leaders must strike the right balance.

CHAPTER 8

CULTIVATING OWNERSHIP

n *Team of Teams*, General Stanley McChrystal uses the metaphor of a gardener to describe the role of a leader. "The gardener cannot actually 'grow' tomatoes, squash, or beans—[the gardener] can only foster an environment in which the plants do so," McChrystal writes. "So it is with leaders."[12]

McChrystal's point is that a leader's job is not to "direct" growth but rather to create the right environment for teams to thrive. Ownership works the same way. One cannot simply tell members of their team to "own more," "take initiative," or "think like a CEO." These statements mean nothing to most attorneys. Instead, much like a gardener must provide soil, water, and sunlight for plants to grow by themselves, managers must think carefully about what factors will encourage attorneys to step into an ownership mindset.

To cultivate this mindset, leaders must *empower* team members to take initiative and solve problems. When attorneys feel empowered, their relationship with the team changes. They no longer see problems as inevitable; instead, they see *solutions* as inevitable. This optimism is not fanciful; if they are all committed to the team's goals and believe they are capable of solving problems along the way, then success always feels within reach.

But that kind of momentum takes time to build. In the last chapter, we explored the manager's role as a teacher. Those one-on-one interactions allow a manager to coach individual attorneys and encourage ownership, little by little. In this chapter, we will zoom out and look for a broader set of best practices to encourage ownership *at scale*—across the entire team or organization. Then we will highlight several pitfalls to avoid, particularly situations where ownership principles are misunderstood, mishandled, or flat-out abused.

Four practices help create this environment of empowerment: delegation with guardrails, de-escalation, risk reinforcement, and—for more senior leaders—a commitment to "teaching the teachers."

DELEGATION WITH GUARDRAILS

Delegation is not just a time-management technique; it is a critical tool for developing more junior attorneys. But knowing where to draw the line between the tasks you keep and those you delegate is not as intuitive as many attorneys believe.

Imagine a company's general counsel assembling a team of in-house attorneys to make legal recommendations about a new business initiative. The GC drafts a list of tasks that will need to get done, such as:

1. Clarifying the team's goals
2. Assembling the work plan and timeline
3. Setting agendas for team meetings
4. Conducting legal research
5. Drafting an outline for recommendations
6. Writing the first draft of recommendations for feedback
7. Completing the final draft and submitting to stakeholders

Now the question is: which tasks should the GC own as team leader, and which should the team members themselves own?

Many managers would draw the line somewhere between #3 and #4. That is, they would mark themselves down as the "owner" for clarifying the team's goals, assembling the work plan and timeline, and setting agendas for team meetings, but they would delegate (i.e., merely be a "reviewer") on the research and drafting phases.

While it is natural for a team leader to think of tasks #1-3 as "management" tasks, we have already poked holes in that thinking. In the previous chapter, for example, we saw that asking a junior team member to draft agendas could be a significant development opportunity. The manager can still review these agendas before they are finalized, but allowing team members to take a "first crack" at such activities encourages them to step up and think about the bigger picture.

In fact, the best practice would be for the manager to own #1—clarifying the team's goals—and then shift into more of a reviewer role for #2-6. By setting the team's goals, we make clear where we want the team to end up. But by delegating #2-6, we grant the team a degree of autonomy to determine precisely *how* they will get from A to B. This autonomy is not unfettered; along the way, managers will set constraints, such as scope limitations and deadlines, and provide support. But these constraints and interventions are the exceptions; the team remains largely in control of execution.

This is a practice known as "delegating with guardrails." Think of it as the happy medium between too much autonomy and too little. On the one hand, if the manager fails to set clear goals or fails to provide appropriate constraints, the team has too much autonomy. This typically results in scope creep (adding more to the project than is necessary), missed deadlines, or even infighting as the team lacks alignment around any single, shared objective. At the other extreme, when a manager becomes too involved in day-to-day execution, the team is robbed of autonomy, and instead of focusing on doing their part to help the team hit its goals, they downshift into a "do what I'm told" mentality.

Again, delegation does not mean the team can do as it pleases. Delegating with guardrails means that managers are still available to help, they still monitor progress, and they still provide feedback and corrections. But wherever possible, managers should avoid doing (or redoing) the team's work.* (And if they must do so, perhaps because time is limited, the manager should go back to the team after the push is over to explain and coach the team as to *why* the manager made those changes.)

Too often, attorneys are afraid to grant the team too much autonomy. We will dive deeper into delegation in Chapter 15,

---

* There is an exception for situations where the manager is required to serve as both a team leader *and* an individual contributor on a team, perhaps due to resource constraints. But if this is the case, that should be spelled out from the beginning, and the manager should be explicit about which tasks will remain with the manager rather than "dabbling" in everyone's work—an excuse for micromanagement.

with even more concrete tactics to find this balance. But for now, keep in mind this maxim: micromanaged teams focus on *avoiding errors*, while well-managed teams focus on *accomplishing goals*. The practice of delegating with guardrails allows managers to strike the right balance.

DEVELOPMENT THROUGH DE-ESCALATION

Unsurprisingly, attorneys who excel in their legal duties are often asked to take on management responsibilities. So it is entirely natural that their team members would seek to benefit from their manager's expertise and experience. As one attorney expressed in a training seminar, "My bosses are smarter than I am in just about every way. So every day, I basically just think about how I can extract as much of their expertise as possible."

Many managers might be flattered to be described this way. But well-intentioned as this sentiment is, attorneys who consistently appeal to their manager's prowess to solve problems do not gain the confidence they need to take ownership.

To help team members build confidence, managers need a thoughtful "de-escalation" strategy. That is, when team members ask for help, a manager's first instinct should be to consider whether the team member *could* solve the problem independently with a nudge in the right direction. If so, instead of answering the question directly, a manager could try to coax the attorney to get there intuitively. For example, the following questions help position a manager as a thought partner:

- "What options have you considered so far?"
- "What else could you try?"

- "What are the pros and cons of that?"
- "What is the worst-case scenario, and what could we do to avoid that?"
- "Have you thought about...?"

That said, there is a time and a place for this. If an associate calls at 11 p.m., desperate for help, and you have an answer that could enable that associate to finish the task and get some rest, by all means, gift wrap the answer and hand it over. Or, if you have an idiosyncratic way of doing things, such as a particular preference for formatting a presentation, do not make your team members guess; simply tell them. But these situations should be the exception, not the rule.

When team members escalate every difficult question to the manager, they do not gain the confidence to tackle new challenges on their own. Through de-escalation, managers can still be supportive coaches without undermining empowerment.

RISK REINFORCEMENT

When team members begin to feel a sense of ownership, they will start making suggestions or asking questions about topics beyond the four corners of their assigned tasks. For example, although assigned to one section of a brief, a litigation associate may have comments about another section. Or an attorney on a deal team may recommend a different strategy for sequencing payouts, even though another attorney is working on those terms.

These attorneys are starting to demonstrate a sense of ownership over the "whole" case (or deal, or client). Managers must fan these flames, because in an instant, they could be snuffed out. For example, other attorneys may initially be put off when a peer has suggestions about "their" areas. They may become defensive, either by lashing out or simply stewing in silence. Sometimes, managers who sense that discomfort might even try to relieve the offended attorney's concern by identifying flaws in the original team member's suggestion and dismissing it.

This kind of protectionism undermines ownership. Remember that psychological safety means feeling comfortable taking risks. When attorneys step outside their lane, they are indeed taking a risk: they do not know how others will react, and if the response is negative, they will steer back into their lane to avoid making the same mistake in the future. Ownership can come and go that quickly.

If you recognize this—that is, if you view these fledgling moments of ownership as attorneys taking *risks*—then your job as the manager is to reinforce that those risks are worthwhile. Fan the flame by praising the contribution. Even if the team member's suggestion is not a particularly good one, a manager must handle the situation delicately. For example, in front of the group, the manager might say, "That's a great question. We've looked at that issue before and found it did not apply because of [x]. But I love that you are asking questions about other sections of the brief. I want everyone to be doing that more often."

By taking the opportunity to applaud the first signs of ownership on a team, a manager sends a clear message that ownership is a team norm. Rewarding those who take these risks helps reinforce that principle, thereby encouraging others to follow their example.

TEACHING THE TEACHERS

The final practice is particularly relevant for those who manage other managers. In Chapter 7, we demonstrated that, for managers, an ownership mentality requires a *teaching* mentality. For those who move into more senior ranks—overseeing other managers—the job becomes exponentially more difficult. Now, rather than merely being teachers themselves, these more senior leaders must teach others how to teach.

This is an entirely new skill, and one that requires just as much thought and discipline. It also requires a different kind of oversight on the senior manager's part. For example, imagine three levels of hierarchy: a senior manager overseeing a junior manager who oversees several team members. The senior manager likely sees the team's final output (namely, the work product) and has regular check-ins with the junior manager. But for most senior managers, this is the beginning and end of their information gathering. Everything they know about the team's performance comes through the filter of the junior manager.

At this point, you hopefully see why this could be problematic. The senior manager might naively think the junior manager is doing a terrific job based on the high-quality output from "the team." But in fact, the junior manager might be destroying team morale with mismanagement. The team members might be burned out. Or, the team members might have no clue what they are doing, but the junior manager covers all the team's mistakes by personally redoing the work the night before the deadline. Yet the senior manager sits in blissful ignorance, naively patting the junior team member on the back and missing critical opportunities for teaching.

In Chapter 17, we will discuss "one-over-one" meetings and other tools to help senior managers keep a pulse on the team. Those tools can help shed light on these blind spots. But once you detect issues with managers you oversee, how do you help them improve?

For senior managers, solving problems with junior managers means recognizing your unique role of "teaching the teachers." You will have to engage the managers you oversee with more detailed questions about their coaching styles and approaches. You should be sharing your own teaching strategies and asking about theirs. When they come to you frustrated about a difficult team member, you should be reminding them of their role as a teacher and helping them work through the situation using the tactics we discussed in Chapter 7. Then, after the junior manager executes your advice, you should follow up to ask how the conversation with the difficult team member went.

In other words, you are responsible for holding your junior managers accountable—not just for their team's legal work, a mere "output"—but also for how those managers are performing as teachers themselves. If they fail to own their role as teachers, they will not build a high-performance team, and you—the senior manager—will ultimately fail to generate the best leverage from the team (or worse, the team will simply quit).

Make clear that you expect a teaching mentality from your junior managers and are there to help. Engage in this conversation regularly. By adopting a "teaching the teachers" mentality, you can exponentially increase your influence and impact across teams. That's the kind of leverage one needs to turn a small practice area into a juggernaut.

PITFALLS IN EXTENDING OWNERSHIP

Before closing our discussion of ownership, we need to address three pitfalls attorneys may experience when trying to put these principles into practice on their teams. First, leaders trying to create a culture of ownership may overlook the role that cultural and other differences play, leading them to a biased set of expectations. Second, leaders may inadvertently "weaponize" ownership if they fail to explain that the best ownership is *collective ownership*. And finally, individuals with an extreme commitment to ownership—often a team's highest performers—may be at risk for burnout if not properly counseled. But each of these risks can be managed thoughtfully.

Ownership Across Differences

We noted earlier that team members who assume ownership are taking a risk, one that requires psychological safety—a theme that comes up repeatedly in this book. In Chapter 3, we also saw that leaders working to build trust and psychological safety have to consider the role that diversity plays, including differences based on gender identity, race, accessibility, background, and more. People bring their differences to work, and if we pretend otherwise, we will not build an inclusive environment where trust thrives.

These same implications carry over to ownership. If someone has had a lifetime of experience being told to "be polite," "don't ruffle feathers," "do as you're told," and other well-meaning but insulating words of caution, it would be unfair to expect that person to suddenly shake off those admonitions upon joining your legal team. They may have past experience of stepping outside their lane and earning only backlash, an experience not easily forgotten.

Women are more likely than men, for example, to experience such repercussions, as are people of color and other underrepresented groups. Unsurprisingly, I never experienced such backlash personally. In fact, I was rewarded most of the time I stepped outside my lane, spoke truth to power, or showed initiative. I know that it would be a mistake to assume my experience is the norm.

Not everyone will readily adopt an ownership mentality. Be prepared for team members to make progress, but not always in a straight line. Sometimes, "one step forward, two steps back" signals not backpedaling but a *retreat to safety*. As a manager, when you see this behavior, ask questions about what you are witnessing and try to better understand the person's unique perspective. Then try to find ways you can help, including leveraging other leaders or in-house resources.

It takes time to build the confidence necessary to achieve true ownership. But with the right support—and the right team environment—any attorney can achieve this milestone.

Weaponizing Ownership

When we talk about junior team members "owning" problems on their teams, even those caused by their manager, it does not diminish the manager's own responsibilities to address such problems. The best ownership is *collective ownership*, where everyone shares responsibility for what happens on their teams and in their organizations. This important nuance sometimes gets lost in ownership training sessions, and the result can be divisive.

To see why, imagine you are a senior partner standing before a group of junior associates lecturing them about your desire for them to "take more ownership." If you're not careful, this lecture might be misinterpreted to suggest that (a) junior associates complain too much, and (b) they are responsible for all the problems (and solutions) on their teams. That is not an empowering message. Far from it. Worse yet, in time, you will start hearing "you lack ownership" used as a weapon in associates' reviews, sometimes as an excuse for more senior attorneys avoiding their own responsibility for mismanagement.

Instead, leaders need to emphasize that ownership is for *everyone*. If there is a problem on the team, then, yes, we hope that all team members, even the junior members, will do what they can to address the problem constructively. But we also expect managers to do the same. (In fact, our expectations for managers are higher, because these expectations are central to the manager's job description.) In this way, the system should have built-in redundancy—no single point of failure. This is a good thing.

But this is not merely a messaging nuance. For more senior leaders, your job is not only to communicate this expectation but *enforce* it. For example, when you hear a manager lament about an attorney who "lacks ownership," interject. Explain that ownership needs to be modeled and taught, not merely criticized. Ask what the manager has done to foster ownership. Offer to be a sounding board. If it becomes clear that the manager is using complaints about others as a way of avoiding responsibility—that is, the manager is not embracing a teaching mentality—then it may be time to reconsider whether that attorney is the right person to lead the team. After all, if we set expectations but never enforce them, they have no meaning.

The "Over-Ownership" Spiral

The final risk is most common with high performers, which is why it is particularly important for leaders to keep in mind. For attorneys who embrace an ownership mentality, life does not *always* smell sweeter. Despite our goal of collective ownership, the results are typically a bit more lopsided in practice. Those who are most willing and able to take ownership may end up, not surprisingly, taking on more responsibilities than others. This is not just true of legal work; it also applies to administrative tasks, team management responsibilities, and more.

Usually, taking ownership has tremendous benefits. Attorneys who take on more responsibility generally learn more, grow faster, and are promoted more quickly. And because they are so good at solving problems on their team, they, by definition, have fewer problems. Win-win, right?

In fact, taken to its extreme, which unfortunately is more common with high performers, "over-ownership" can create two potential risks. The first is burnout. If one is always volunteering for tasks and putting the team's goals first, such a person may end up in an unhealthy situation. This can be exacerbated by managers who are ignorant of their team members' true work-life balance and overall mental health. That is why much of this book is dedicated to helping managers develop closer relationships with their team members (so they have the trust necessary to discuss concerns like burnout more openly) and implementing tools, such as surveys, to monitor organizational health (as we will discuss in Chapter 17). But managers should also avoid relying too heavily on their highest performers. They must keep careful track of the work assigned to team members—not just the legal work, but other responsibilities such as event planning, recruiting, and more—to ensure the load is balanced across the team as much as possible.

Be mindful of gender dynamics here as well. Many legal teams have an unfortunate habit of assigning administrative tasks or responsibilities for team social events to women on the team, a pattern that is noticeable, condescending, and undermines morale. Consider rotating responsibilities to make clear that *everyone* is expected to carry the water.

Second, individuals with an extreme sense of ownership can have a hard time letting go of a problem. For example, losing sleep while spiraling on ways to untangle a difficult problem at work can happen to anyone, but if it happens over and over, it may be time to take a step back. An ownership mentality should be encouraged, but with reasonable *limits*. In other words, yes, it is healthy to consider what *you* can do to address problems in your workplace, but at the end of the day, you cannot solve *every* problem or change *every* mind. If you do not acknowledge this limitation—if you internalize every team failure as a personal failure—you risk more than just burnout; you risk a spiral of self-doubt. This loss of confidence can do serious damage. All managers should be aware of and be watching out for those who need this reminder.

An ownership mentality is just that: a mentality. It reflects the belief that you can take *action* with respect to the problems around you and the willingness to do so. But it does not transform you into a superhero. By all means, commit yourself to turning complaints into action. But do not let your commitment to ownership jeopardize your happiness, your self-worth, or your mental health.

When team members are willing to take more initiative—to own the team's goals—that commitment begins to manifest everywhere. They support and help each other. They sharpen each other's ideas. And they become more engaged in their work over-all, since they share a deeper commitment to the team.

This commitment also can result in something new: team con-flict. If you care enough about something, you are willing to fight for it. But conflict is not a bad word on legal teams. In fact, it is a point of great leverage.

High-performance teams require productive conflict to fuel their growth. But along the way, destructive conflicts will ignite as well, threatening to derail the team. That is the minefield we must navigate next.

PART 3

PRODUCTIVE CONFLICT

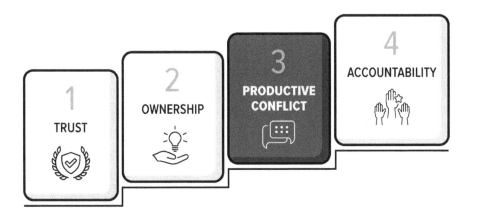

CHAPTER 9

IRON SHARPENS IRON

Productive conflict strengthens our teams. Even those who have no intention of setting foot in a courtroom understand the value of the adversarial process: a thoughtful debate between attorneys can unlock valuable insights and improve every aspect of what we do.

The good news is that we do not have to "do" anything to generate productive conflict. Once you establish trust and ownership, productive conflict is an inevitable byproduct, like a chemical reaction with formulaic consequences. Trust encourages people to bring authenticity to a conversation, including their own opinions, and enables them to share those opinions without fear of ridicule. Ownership then gives people a *reason* to do so: when they care deeply about the team's goals—deeply enough to take action when they see something that can be improved—they will then share their concerns or suggestions even when the issue is not confined to their "silo" of work. Put those ingredients together and, *voila*, productive conflict unfolds.

The bad news is that virtually every productive conflict teeters on a precipice. With a push in the wrong direction, it can easily transform into a destructive conflict, one that tears at the fabric of trust within a team and sends people retreating into self-protection. This is why ownership can so easily unravel: stepping outside of one's lane—a good thing for lawyers with an ownership mentality—can cause friction. If that friction is left to fester, the environment can turn toxic. It is the job of every team member, not just the manager, to keep productive conflicts from turning destructive.

The first step is understanding why productive conflicts become destructive. This chapter will focus on that problem and explain how an attorney's most trusted tools for conflict resolution often fail when needed most. Then, in Chapter 10, we will explore the psychology of conflict. Finally, Chapters 11 and 12 will focus on tactics for overcoming emotional obstacles and other common deadlocks, with practical advice for navigating these sticky situations with your peers, managers, and other team members.

WHEN CONFLICT BECOMES A FOUR-LETTER WORD

Before we dive deeper, we should be clear about the kinds of conflicts we aim to address over the next few chapters. Attorneys who disagree with each other are not necessarily engaged in a "conflict" that calls for an advanced degree in conflict resolution. When attorneys comment on each other's legal work, for example, that might provoke thoughtful discussion, but usually not intense conflict. Redlines are rarely battlegrounds.

We are interested in deeper disagreements that are not resolved with a simple "Accept Change" button. These conflicts might relate to legal matters but just as often relate to organizational issues. For example, attorneys might find themselves engaged in conflicts over:

- Who will take the next batch of document review
- The best way to approach a discovery dispute
- The optimal deal structure for a client
- The right strategy for negotiating deal terms
- Who should have a speaking role at a hearing or client meeting

Conflicts can become even more challenging for senior leaders, such as partners with broader business responsibilities. For example:

- How to handle a conflict of interest between the clients of two different partners
- Deciding to ramp hiring up or down
- Whether to spend more on training programs
- Setting compensation and awarding raises

And the stickiest conflicts of all tend to be interpersonal conflicts, such as when animosity arises because one attorney interrupts another, or when a junior associate is frustrated with a more senior attorney's micromanagement. These are the conflicts where the skills described over the next several chapters come into play.

Next, we need to be clear about the difference between productive and destructive conflicts. Below is a table outlining these characteristics. Review the two lists and consider which of these behaviors you have seen on your teams.

SIGNS OF PRODUCTIVE CONFLICT	SIGNS OF DESTRUCTIVE CONFLICT
Challenging ideas	Challenging people
Asking questions with genuine curiosity	Stating opinions disguised as questions
Listening and considering other viewpoints before speaking	Using the time while someone else speaks to plan one's next comment
Assuming others' intentions are positive—to help the team	Assuming others' intentions are self-centered—to help themselves
Openly discussing difficult subjects that affect the group	Avoiding important issues, i.e., the "elephant in the room"

While the difference between productive and destructive conflict might seem clear on paper, the lines can become quite blurry in practice. The difference between challenging "ideas" and challenging "people," for example, can be a matter of perception. Those perceptions can be influenced by a wide variety of factors, from personality styles to life experience to past scars from previous interactions with particular team members.

All of this means that you may be engaging in what you *believe* is a lively debate with another attorney, only to find out later that the other attorney thought your behavior was antagonistic. These misunderstandings can (and do) happen every day on legal teams.

We have to embrace this subjectivity. To extend the previous section's lesson on ownership, you have to "own" your role in conflicts, looking for ways you can help keep the conflict productive *regardless* of whether you believe others are to blame for causing the conflict, or even if you believe others are being too sensitive or unfair in their perceptions. In conflict resolution, these beliefs are irrelevant. What matters is that the conflict exists, and you are in a position to set things right.

PROTECTING THE RELATIONSHIP

To manage disagreements effectively, we have to keep in mind that there are two goals in every conflict. First, there is the obvious goal: resolving the substantive dispute. For example, attorneys may have a conflict over litigation strategy, the optimal deal structure for a client, how to handle a conflict of interest, who should be first chair at the next hearing, whether to hire additional associates, and so on. Ultimately, a decision has to be made; that decision is the means of resolving the substance of the conflict.

But the most adept leaders acknowledge a second goal in conflicts, one that is more subtle and often overlooked: *protecting the relationship*. After all, team members have to keep working together long after the substance of the disagreement is resolved, and strong teams can spiral into factions if a conflict tears at the trust they developed. For some attorneys, getting to the "right" answer is all that matters—reflecting the kind of binary thinking to which lawyers are accustomed. If people are upset along the way, that is unfortunate, but necessary. "I don't have time to worry about bruised egos," more than one partner has told me over the years.

While this view of conflicts may sound cold, it has a certain logic. After all, when two people want different things, and the only way for one person to "win" is for the other to "lose," then without fail, someone will be upset at the outcome. In game theory (a branch of mathematics), this outcome is known as a "zero-sum game," because one person's "wins" are equal to another's "losses" (the sum of which is zero). If you view a conflict as a zero-sum game, the situation quickly turns adversarial. And while most attorneys have no *desire* to hurt a colleague's feelings, some are willing to sacrifice people's feelings if that is the only way to get to the right answer.

Thankfully, this is a false choice. We do not have to choose between the "right answer" and "protecting the relationship." In fact, there are two mistakes with this mindset. One is thinking that every conflict has a binary answer, when in fact, conflict resolution experts understand that the best stalemates are broken through more creative solutions—something we will explore extensively in Chapter 12. But the other mistake is in underestimating how the decision-making process—that is, everything *but* the decision itself—affects the relationship.

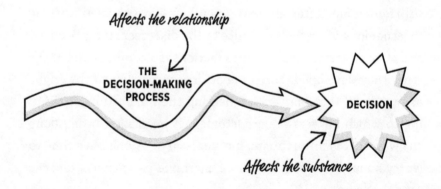

It turns out that people are much more likely to accept an outcome if they feel the process was fair, even if the outcome was objectively *less favorable* to them. Studies in social psychology, such as those by Jerald Greenberg of Ohio State University, showed this phenomenon in action during experiments about procedural justice, but the ramifications go much further.[13] If people feel that they have been heard, that their ideas were respected, and that the ultimate decision took into account all sides, then they are much more likely to accept the outcome, even when it goes against their positions.

In other words, the process is just as important as the final decision. A thoughtful process is the spoonful of sugar that helps the decision go down, even when that decision is unpopular. Establishing a healthy process means giving people a chance to be heard and showing that you are genuinely interested in all perspectives. This small gesture can have a tremendous impact. By mentally distinguishing the process from the decision, it becomes easier to see why you do not necessarily have to choose between a suboptimal decision and preserving the relationship.

And just as importantly, a thoughtful process actually yields *better* decisions. More perspectives can help sharpen ideas, which is why we want productive conflict in the first place. Senior attorneys can also have a habit of focusing *too much* on the "big picture" and missing nuances that only those who are working in the weeds will spot. A process that gives everyone a chance to be heard ensures these nuances float to the surface.

A thoughtful process is not a panacea; sometimes, people will still find the outcome difficult to stomach. But leaders should not approach difficult decisions like "ripping off a band-aid," thinking that a quick decision will avoid turmoil. This abruptness will likely cause *more* damage, not less.

This lesson is not just for managers and other decision-makers. Junior associates, for example, will face all manner of conflicts with their peers that they have to resolve on their own, without appealing for help from a manager.

OVERLY-RATIONAL ACTORS

As attorneys, we are well-trained in the art of argument. We conduct thorough research, gather facts and evidence, structure our ideas carefully, and present our points methodically. These are our best tools for resolving *legal* conflicts. Yet when it comes to *interpersonal* conflicts, these tools often fail us.

Researchers have conducted many studies about the most effective tactics for influencing colleagues. That is what we are typically trying to do in a conflict: change another person's mind. In one study, rational persuasion—the tactic attorneys are often most comfortable using—actually sparked one of the highest levels of *resistance*.[14] In fact, rational persuasion generated roughly the same pushback one would get from simply ordering someone around (called "legitimating"). Yet it was by far the most deployed tactic, despite these shortcomings.

TACTIC	FREQUENCY OF USE	RESULT		
		RESISTANCE ("NO!")	COMPLIANCE ("FINE.")	COMMITMENT ("YES!")
1. Rational persuasion	54%	47%	30%	23%
2. Legitimating	13%	44%	56%	0%
3. Personal appeals	7%	25%	33%	42%
4. Offering an exchange	7%	25%	33%	42%
5. Ingratiation	6%	41%	28%	31%
6. Pressure	6%	56%	41%	3%
7. Building coalitions	3%	53%	44%	3%
8. Inspirational appeals	2%	0%	10%	90%
9. Consultation	2%	18%	27%	55%

This does not mean we should stop employing facts and reasoning. By all means, in a conflict, explain your view as clearly as possible using all available information. But the toughest deadlocks between team members are rarely resolved by one person throwing additional facts and arguments at the other person. If that were enough to settle the disagreement, the conflict would barely register on our radar.

For stickier, more entrenched conflicts, we have to set aside our beloved logical weapons and look for other explanations for why this conflict is occurring. Only then can we do our part to address the true cause of the deadlock.

This process begins with unpacking the psychology of conflicts. Destructive conflicts occur not simply because people disagree but because of *how* they approach disagreements. In the next chapter, we will learn how to spot these differences in ourselves and others.

CHAPTER 10

CONFLICT STYLES

n the 1960s, not only did most managers think of themselves as natural collaborators, but they had the data to back it up. Psychologists had recently begun putting together self-assessments related to conflict behavior and testing them in the wild, and sure enough, over 90% of managers received scores indicating they were highly "collaborative" and not at all conflict "avoiding."[15]

But in the 1970s, two doctoral students, Ken Thomas and Ralph Kilmann, crossed paths in a behavioral science class at UCLA. The course taught them to become experts in quantitative assessments of human behavior, and they spotted a serious flaw in these early versions of conflict style assessments: the questions reeked of bias. The idea that collaboration was "good" and conflict avoidance was "bad" had influenced—or to be more accurate, tainted—the assessment questions, such that most self-respecting managers answered in whatever pointed toward the "socially desirable" image of a collaborative conflict style. "Their subordinates, of course, experienced those same managers very differently," Kilmann wrote.[16]

Once they found the bug, Thomas and Kilmann set out to squash it. They created a new assessment, the Thomas-Kilmann Conflict Instrument, or TKI, that removed this bias. Once they did—*poof*—the delusion went up in smoke. The truth, it turned out, was that only 17% of people have a natural predisposition to "collaborating" in conflict.[17] More importantly, there is nothing *wrong* with that outcome. Humans have just as much diversity in how they handle conflict as they do in other aspects of their personality (like Social Styles).

In this chapter, we'll explore the psychology of conflicts through the lens of TKI, which to this day remains one the of the most prominent tools for analyzing conflict styles. By understanding these psychological patterns—both in ourselves and others—attorneys can navigate minefields with colleagues far more effectively.

THE FIVE CONFLICT MODES

The TKI examines conflict modes across two dimensions: "assertiveness," which refers to how strongly people pursue their own concerns, and "cooperativeness," referring to how strongly people work to satisfy the concerns of others. At first glance, these concepts might seem mutually exclusive, but they are not. People can, for example, look for a way to address both their interests and the interest of others—a win-win scenario. People can also pursue neither—avoiding the conflict entirely.

The TKI includes a thirty-question assessment about one's approach to conflicts and then plots the person on a chart like the one below:

CONFLICT MODES OVERVIEW

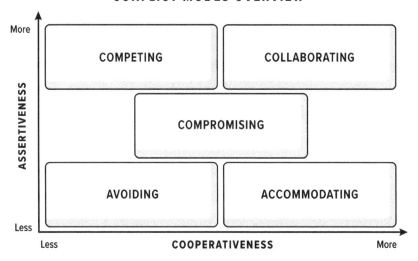

As you can see, there are five possible conflict modes: avoiding, accommodating, compromising, competing, and collaborating. Like other assessments, you can purchase access to the official TKI and complete the thirty-question assessment by yourself or with your team members.* This can serve as an excellent team-building tool, spurring conversations as people share their conflict styles and examples of how those styles manifest in practice.

Even without access to the full assessment, you can still understand the basic framework and the five conflict modes. Below is a high-level summary of each. As you read the summaries, consider which mode you use most often and most naturally at work. Everyone is capable of operating in all five modes at different times, and we can deliberately change our behavior in conflicts

---

* You can access official versions of the TKI from Kilmann Diagnostics or the Myers-Briggs Company.

depending on the situation. (In fact, learning how to do that effectively is one of our goals.) But first, attorneys have to take stock of their natural instincts in a workplace conflict.

In addition to considering your own conflict mode, think about your colleagues as you proceed through this list. Each summary includes tips for how you might tune your approach based on a colleague's style.

Avoiding

In the lower left corner of the chart, we have conflict avoidance. In Western culture, we tend to think of this as a negative trait. But avoiding conflict goes hand in hand with picking one's battles, a useful tactic in many situations. Avoiding conflict can also be a protective choice, ensuring that one "lives to fight another day," rather than spending social capital on trivial issues. But like all the conflict modes we will discuss, conflict avoidance can have negative repercussions if overused: conflicts we evade for too long tend to fester and erupt if given enough time.

When dealing with someone who is conflict-avoidant, the best strategy can be to reduce the appearance of conflict, such as working to get others on board first before approaching the conflict-avoidant target. It may also help to build momentum, starting with less contentious items first and saving the toughest issues for the end. These small tweaks can yield a smoother path through an otherwise difficult conversation.

Accommodating

Those with "accommodating" conflict styles tend to be willing to sacrifice their own interests to satisfy the concerns of others. As a result, accommodating people tend to be seen as generous and selfless, building their social capital. It becomes easier to let down one's guard with accommodating colleagues because of their genuine interest in helping you achieve your goals. Of course, while this may allow some immediate conflicts to be resolved, it can also lead to problems later, since the accommodating person may still have needs or concerns that were not addressed. This can fuel resentment.

You may wonder if an accommodating conflict style is incompatible with the practice of law, as though an attorney with this inclination would not be vigorous in pursuing a client's interests. Not true. I have taught countless law students and lawyers who scored high on the accommodating conflict mode and were nevertheless highly successful in their careers. This is because people tend to behave differently—more assertively—when negotiating for a third party (like a client) than they do when negotiating for their own personal interests. Remember, conflict modes help us understand one's natural approach and comfort level in conflicts; these are not rigid mindsets.

When working with an accommodating person, be clear about your issues and concerns; they want to help. But avoid taking advantage of the individual's generosity. You may reach a superficial decision that appears to be in your favor, only to have your counterpart chip away at your agreement later. In negotiation theory, we call this a "fragile deal," the kind of thing that happens when an acquirer is pressed into paying a higher price for a company than they originally intended, which then leads them to seek out any excuse in due diligence to escape their commitment. Team members may do the same thing when they are pushed into accepting an outcome that, deep down, leaves them feeling unsatisfied or unsupported.

Compromising

At the middle of the TKI grid lies the "compromising" mode. A compromising approach tends to involve "meeting in the middle" or "splitting the difference." While this can be an expedient way to reach a deal, it can lead to subpar outcomes. In fact, the title of a popular negotiation book—*Never Split the Difference*, by Chris Voss—serves as a warning against this way of thinking.[18] When you resolve a conflict by meeting in the middle, you might save time, but you miss out on other, more creative solutions that could leave *both* sides more satisfied. (We'll talk through a detailed example when we discuss "the Orange Story" in Chapter 12.) Compromisers also risk exploitation because their counterparts might intentionally ask for something more extreme—known as "aggressive anchoring"—to ensure that any "middle ground" solution ends up being more favorable to them.

For those trying to resolve a dispute with someone prone to compromise, be mindful of these dynamics. Look for opportunities to slow the process down and dig deeper into root causes, which may yield more robust long-term solutions. Then, if time runs short, you can still fall back to an expedient, "meet in the middle" solution.

Competing

At the top left of the grid, we have the "competing" mode, where individuals tend to be assertive about their own interests and less interested in helping others achieve their goals. Competing individuals are more likely to view conflicts as zero-sum games, where one person wins and the other loses. Although some might view this as selfish—a negative connotation—this mode is also consistent with "standing up for one's rights," a potentially noble principle that lawyers understand well.

But competing behavior can result in tunnel vision. By focusing solely on one's own interests, a person may fail to realize more creative solutions, similar to the risk we discussed for compromisers who focus on expediency. Also, great negotiators know that the best way to close a deal is to explain how your proposal satisfies the *other person's* interests; after all, people do not much care to hear why your proposal is good for *you*. People with highly competitive conflict modes often overlook this tactic and become too entrenched in their own way of thinking, making them less influential.

When a colleague has a competitive style, your best approach is to find ways to make the person feel like a "winner." For example, when making a compromise, call attention to what you are giving up, even if not that important to you, since anything you "lose" is considered a "win" by a competitive person. And if the competitive person makes a mistake—such as referring to facts that turn out to be wrong or losing one's cool—look for ways to let the competitive person save face, rather than calling attention to those missteps. This is because, when cornered, competitive individuals can become more stubborn, refusing to yield even if it means taking the entire team down with them, an outcome that benefits no one.

Collaborating

The final mode, "collaborating," refers to those who pursue *both* their interests and the interests of others wherever possible. They like to look for "win-win" scenarios, relying on creative problem solving to come up with novel solutions. For example, they might dig deeper into the root causes of a conflict to address the problem at its source, or they may connect the dots between this conflict and other issues, thereby unlocking a bigger-picture solution that addresses many problems at once.

There are obvious advantages in this approach, but the truth is, no conflict mode is ideal, and even collaborative approaches can have disadvantages. For example, collaborative individuals tend to look at conflicts like a puzzle, hoping to find the perfect solution where everyone can be satisfied. But in many conflicts, finding the "perfect" solution is either impossible or simply not worth the time. Not every conflict warrants this kind of attention. Also, collaborative solutions that address "root causes," while perhaps helpful for the team's long-term growth, may require getting more people involved, adding complexity and slowing down decision-making. In some situations, people may find that such a cure is more costly than the disease.

When working with an individual who operates in the collaborating mode, it's best to mirror their style if you can. Be open about your goals and show an interest in theirs by asking thoughtful questions. Proceed with an open mind, ready to brainstorm creative solutions. (Collaborative people value having a strong thought partner.) But along the way, watch the clock. Avoid spending too much time trying to find the "perfect" answer and, where appropriate, encourage this person to adopt a solution that optimizes not just for everyone's interests but also for efficiency.

———

Whatever your TKI mode, it is to your advantage to learn how to employ *all five* modes depending on the situation. In my negotiation courses, I encourage law students to identify their natural conflict style and look for opportunities to try different approaches, thereby expanding their comfort zone and their toolkit. After a semester of negotiation exercises, my students overwhelmingly find they are more comfortable in conflict—and more willing to negotiate for things—than they were when they started.

But when the subject of the conflict concerns one's own career—such as pushing a manager for better opportunities, promotion, or compensation—there may be more complex dynamics at play. Next, we will address this special class of conflicts.

PROMOTING EQUITY IN CONFLICTS

In many organizations, especially law firms with a "free market" system,* attorneys are expected to be their own advocates for career opportunities. This can be difficult for those who are conflict-averse, but one's conflict mode is not the only factor at play here. Conflicts that involve self-advocacy are unique because many people who are perfectly comfortable pushing for the interests of a third party (like a client) find it much more difficult to advocate for their own personal interests. In her research at Carnegie Mellon University, Linda Babcock and others found that this phenomenon is especially common among women (and additional underrepresented groups) because they are more likely than men to encounter social backlash when they advocate for themselves; this backlash then leads them to shy away from pursuing their own interests in the future, a contributing factor to disparate outcomes in the workplace.[19]

As the saying goes, the squeaky wheel gets the oil. When people consistently avoid conflict, they can miss out on opportunities,

---

* The "free market" system generally allows associates to choose their practice areas or their matters, within reason, by building their own network of senior associates and partners and seeking out preferred assignments.

from financial opportunities, such as bonuses and raises, to experiential opportunities, such as having a bigger role in a litigation or deal.

Telling those who have lived this experience that they need to "be stronger advocates for themselves" misses the broader lesson from this research. These barriers are systemic; that is, they reflect accumulated patterns and practices that are larger than any one individual. The people best positioned to address these barriers are those who have the most authority in that system— i.e., managers and executives. Rather than expect others to advocate for themselves, we as leaders need to own our responsibility to advocate for *others*.

For those in leadership positions, there are three additional ways we can contribute. The first is coaching—but not in the way you might think. Encouraging someone to "speak up" more in meetings may be a well-intentioned piece of advice, but that advice is often provided disproportionately to women, reinforcing gender stereotypes. The suggestion is also not particularly actionable, much like telling someone who struggles with taking initiative to "take more initiative." People who lack the confidence to speak up in meetings feel this way for a reason, such as the experience of social backlash discussed earlier; telling someone *not* to feel this way is unhelpful. People cannot simply "forget" about the subtle and systemic backlash they have experienced over the course of a lifetime.

Instead, start with positive reinforcement. For example, when a typically quiet colleague speaks up in a meeting to provide a contrary view, be vocal that you appreciate the contribution— whether or not you agree with that particular suggestion. This aligns with the advice in Chapter 8, when we discussed reinforcing the early steps that colleagues take in the path of ownership.

If you do notice a situation in which you think the attorney missed an opportunity to be more vocal, approach the issue as a dialogue—not a lecture. That is, rather than tell the colleague to "step up" next time, ask why the attorney did not do so *this time*, and listen carefully to the answer. Do not make assumptions. By opening a dialogue, you may learn more about your colleague's reasoning, the person's conflict style, and even the person's history with conflicts, allowing you to be a more thoughtful mentor. And if the person is not comfortable opening up to you in this way, do not push. Remember, trust takes time to build.

The second way to help reduce the cycle of backlash is to ensure you do not engage in backlash yourself. From time to time, your team members may call attention to issues or ideas that put you on the defensive. This is a critical test for your leadership. Even subtle clues that you are frustrated by their input can undermine your goal of creating space for productive conflict. And in more extreme cases where you believe that a colleague needs to pick one's battles better, by all means, consider coaching, but first gut-check whether unconscious bias may be playing a role, i.e., whether you would give the same counsel to a colleague with a different identity or background.

Finally, leaders should understand that people are more willing to engage in conflicts when they understand the rules of engagement. For example, Babcock and other researchers conducted a controlled experiment where participants won a certain initial amount of money and then had the chance to negotiate for more. They found that women were far less likely than men to ask for more money *unprompted*, but when women and men were explicitly *told* they could ask for more money, those disparities closed.[20] Essentially, by reducing the ambiguity about whether the situation was negotiable, negotiation confidence increased.

This has implications far beyond compensation. Even normal, everyday interactions between team members can be opportunities for healthy conflict, whether it be challenging each other's ideas or deciding which team member will get the plush assignment. Leaders can reduce disparate outcomes by being explicit about wanting to hear from *everyone*.*

For example, in a team meeting, rather than simply asking for input on a tricky issue and creating a free-for-all (where the loudest voices typically dominate), consider starting with an "around the horn" approach. Go one by one around the table, giving each person sixty seconds to share overall reactions. Once everyone has shared, allow a free discussion. This single tweak tends to work wonders for getting input from otherwise timid colleagues, and over time, they build greater confidence and trust with the group.

By taking into account differences in conflict styles, attorneys can ensure the best ideas come to the surface, regardless of a colleague's rank or background. Nothing could be more important for unlocking the potential of a high-performance team.

———

* As a case in point, a study of law students at the University of Virginia showed that men were more likely than women to dominate class discussions when participation was voluntary; those disparities closed when professors called on students systematically. See Molly Bishop Shadel, Sophie Trawalter, and J.H. Verkerke, "Gender Differences in Law School Classroom Participation: The Key Role of Social Context," *Virginia Law Review* 108 (February 2022): 30–54, https://www.virginialawreview.org/articles/gender-differences-in-law-school-classroom-participation-the-key-role-of-social-context/.

Understanding the psychology of conflicts can make anyone—not just attorneys—more effective in managing these tricky situations. But for attorneys, these lessons are particularly important because so much of our training is geared toward rational arguments. By considering the psychological angles, we become far more attuned to our colleagues' motives and needs—not to mention growing more aware of our own unhealthy habits.

Of course, understanding conflict styles is just the first step. Next, we will talk tactics, starting with techniques for addressing the kinds of obstacles that even the most battle-hardened attorneys find utterly exhausting: emotional conflicts.

CHAPTER 11

EMOTIONAL OBSTACLES

n a heated conflict, we have all witnessed someone—or been the someone—saying, "Stop being so emotional."

The exact wording varies, but the impetus is the same. "Don't take this so personally," some might say. Or the more subtle version: "Can we please just stay focused?"

When I hear team members use these lines on an emotional colleague, all I can think is, "Has that *ever* worked?" Has anyone ever responded, "You're absolutely right. I *am* being too emotional—thank you for that suggestion," and then transformed into a calm, rational actor?

Humans do not have an emotional off switch. Nor do we have absolute control over how our bodies respond to stress. In a conflict—or any stressful situation—our autonomic nervous system kicks into high gear. It signals the adrenal glands to release epinephrine (i.e., adrenaline) and cortisol, hormones that prepare our bodies for the fight-or-flight response we talked about in Chapter 2. These hormones have a measurable effect on our brains' ability to process information. Rather than the thoughtful, open-minded colleagues we'd like to be, these hormones turn us into one-track minds, focusing on whatever triggered the stress—the threat at hand—and boxing out other cognitive impulses.

If you are watching closely in these moments, you can even spot physical signs of transformation in a person. Clenched jaws, tense muscles, balled-up fists, heavy breathing through flared nostrils—these are the subtle but visible cues of stress and heightened emotions, especially anger and resentment. These are also the warning signs of a conflict turning destructive. Unfortunately, people in the middle of a heated disagreement often get so wrapped up in the discussion that they miss these signs in colleagues, and even in themselves.

Managing emotional situations requires considerable awareness and a careful approach. In this chapter, we will discuss ways to get back on track when conflicts take an emotional turn.

MANAGING YOUR EMOTIONS FIRST

Anyone who has flown in an airplane is familiar with the safety reminder that, if the cabin depressurizes and oxygen masks drop from the ceiling, you should put on your mask before attempting to help other passengers. This is good advice; in the time it might take you to help your neighbors, you could lose consciousness from the loss of oxygen. At that point, you're not going to be much help to anyone.

The same holds true in stressful conflicts. You cannot help an emotional colleague if you are caught up in the emotional tension as well; you need to focus on yourself first. But we tend to over-look our own emotions, either because we do not notice our heat rising or because we think we can simply ignore the alarm bells and stay focused on "the issue at hand" in the conflict. Biologically speaking, that is a tall order; the systems in your body that manage stressful situations work without conscious thought.

Imagine having an IV in your arm during a conflict, watching it pump mind-altering drugs into your system, and then trying to overcome the effects with sheer force of will. That is not a good plan.

Rather than ignore these emotional and physical changes or pretend they are not affecting us, we instead need to *increase* our awareness so that we can make adjustments to avoid letting them affect our judgment and our actions. If we do not make these changes—if we instead pretend our brain is the same as it's always been—we will inevitably make mistakes: we will say things we regret, we will overlook social cues, or we will simply miss opportunities to help get the situation back on track. These mistakes are all avoidable.

The process begins with increasing our self-awareness so that we notice our triggers. Some triggers are universal: a sudden loud noise or being struck by a falling object will send even the calmest person into a fight-or-flight response. But those are unlikely to occur in an office environment, so we are interested in more subtle triggers.

For example, below is a list of common stress triggers at work. As you read this list, you may think, *Wouldn't everyone find these situations stressful?* While that may be true to a degree, when we talk about "knowing your triggers," it means looking for situations where you are more likely to have a disproportionate stress

152 · ALL RISE

reaction compared to the average person. Think of these like pet peeves, but on a more emotional level. Consider if any of these triggers resonate with you in particular:

- Betrayal, e.g., a supportive colleague turns against you
- Rejection, e.g., a colleague dismisses your suggestion out of hand
- Injustice, e.g., a manager treats you differently than someone else
- Exclusion, e.g., you notice there is an "in-group"—and you're not a member
- Criticism, e.g., a piece of feedback seems to attack not just your ideas but your abilities or character
- Loss of autonomy, e.g., someone micromanages your every move
- Condescension, e.g., someone speaks to you like you are a child
- Disrespect, e.g., someone rudely interrupts you or you are made to wait, wasting your time

Note that this is just a partial list. Triggers can be even more specific and reflect someone's particular experience or insecurities.

By better understanding your triggers, you can reduce their impact. This is a process sometimes called taking a personal "inventory." If you are honest with yourself and own your triggers, you are much more likely to recognize when they are activated in real time and avoid them taking hold.

Environmental factors can also make our triggers more sensitive. For example, some people seem on edge when they miss lunch or haven't had their morning coffee. Lack of sleep, food, and other biological factors affect our moods, and pretending you are immune to these needs is not going to make your blood sugar stabilize *itself*. All of this should be considered when taking your personal inventory.

Achieving this kind of real-time awareness is a great advantage, but it is easier said than done. When frustrated in a conflict, we like to think our indignation is righteous. All our thoughts turn to why the *other* person is off base. In other words, we tend *not* to think about the possibility that—even if the colleague is indeed wrong—we nevertheless might be reacting more sensitively to the situation because it hits a particular nerve with us.

If you develop sufficient awareness to notice when you are feeling triggered, there are several concrete things you can do to take control of the situation. The first, as we hinted above, is to pause. For some, even one deep breath can be enough to avoid a career-limiting move. A longer break can be even more impactful. This need not be a dramatic request. Frame it as a bathroom break. Pretend to take a phone call. Go feed the meter. Or, if you are running the meeting and have the ability to control the agenda, consider saying, "We've surfaced a lot of good points so far. Let's digest this and come back together tomorrow for a final decision." There are plenty of ways to make such breaks seem natural.

If you cannot leave the room, there are subtle mindfulness techniques that can have a similar effect. For example, some PTSD sufferers manage spikes of stress by taking a moment to identify four distinct sounds in a room, a mental exercise that shifts one's focus away from the triggering event. If you did the same thing in a meeting, your colleagues would likely never notice.

Taking a mental break can do wonders for unlocking the conflict. It allows people to calm down and start seeing the situation from different angles, coming up with better approaches. This is not a coincidence; this is what happens when the cortisol and adrenaline are reabsorbed, loosening their grip on our cognitive function. As the tunnel vision dissipates, we become genuinely more effective thought partners once again.

Some attorneys dismiss these tools as "soft," as though one's mental fortitude is all a person needs to manage stress. They even scorn others who are "unable to handle the stress" of the job. While it is true that attorneys must face—and be able to manage—stressful situations, it is equally true that stress management is a skill that can be learned and practiced, not simply some fixed personality trait. This is all coachable.

And for those attorneys who think themselves "above" stress management, a word of warning: in my experience, those who most aggressively roll their eyes in conversations about managing stress tend, ironically, to be the same ones who need it most (according to their colleagues).

There is no perfect recipe for managing your emotions. It takes awareness, iteration, and practice to build this skill. Individuals may also have special circumstances, such as mood disorders, traumatic histories, or other factors that make it more difficult to stay effective in a stressful conflict. Whatever your situation, consider what steps you can take to find the most productive path forward, and be open to feedback from colleagues and coaching from experts, where appropriate. The only wrong path here is to pretend you have no need for these skills; to do so is to believe you are not human.

HANDLING OTHERS' EMOTIONS

Once you have a better handle on your own emotions—that is, to quote your friendly airline safety video, "once your oxygen mask is properly situated over your nose and mouth"—then you can address the emotions of your fellow team members.

Hopefully, it's clear by this point why telling a colleague to "stop being so emotional" is perhaps the *worst* thing you could say in a heated conflict. This dismissive remark suggests that you think your colleague's emotions are unjustified and that this person has lost control. That is a brutal combination of calling someone irrational and weak at the same time. Given how seriously we take our ability to think clearly, you can bet most lawyers would take offense at this suggestion. If anything, it would only serve to escalate the conflict.

Instead, when your colleague is emotional, you have to address the person's emotions directly and sensitively, not dismissively. The classic example of this principle in action comes not from a law firm or even a workplace at all, but from romantic life.

Suppose your partner comes home one day, sits down in a huff, and unloads a long story about the terrible boss who is driving the entire team bananas with disorganization. How will you respond? Will you point your partner to Chapter 6, Scenario #1, where we discuss ways to take ownership over a manager's disorganization? Will you offer suggestions on how your partner can step up to organize the team meeting and help keep things on track?

If you do, you might find yourself eating dinner alone.

People who are visibly frustrated do not want a lecture; they want someone who understands what they are feeling. This is why your partner will push back on your suggestions even if they have merit. The problem is that you have jumped straight to problem-solving mode and ignored the emotional field. You need to approach the situation differently—with empathy and active listening first—until the person is ready to switch to a more rational discussion.

The same model applies to conflicts with team members at the office. Someone's emotional state may seem like a barrier to resolving the conflict. I prefer to view those emotions as the *key* to resolution. Think of emotions like *data*; it is our job to interpret the data and understand what it is trying to tell us. When people are emotional, it's as though they are flashing giant neon signs pointing to some deeper issue that is important to them. Imagine playing poker and seeing someone fidget with anxiety; just as these tells might be used to understand someone's cards, a person's emotional reaction can act like a beacon, calling your attention to an underlying concern. Your job then becomes finding out what it is and addressing that concern.

For example, many years ago, I was sitting in a corporate acquisition conversation that was going off the rails. The acquirer's representatives were asking due diligence questions of the COO for the company being acquired, and they were becoming visibly frustrated with the COO's answers. But the COO failed to notice that the questions had become tinged with frustration. Instead of digging into this emotional response, he kept focusing on the substantive diligence issues, seemingly ticking boxes off a list. If the COO had only noticed his counterparts' visible frustration and addressed it directly using the techniques we will discuss in a moment, the deal might have stayed on track. He might have learned that the acquirer felt his answers were coming off as evasive, and he might have stopped, taken a step back, and looked for ways to rebuild trust before it slipped through his fingers. But he ignored their emotions, kept his focus on the deal terms, and the deal died.

So how should we address colleagues when emotions are high? As we hinted earlier in the example about your partner's difficult day at the office, your two most important tools for emotional situations are empathy and active listening. In a nutshell, empathy is about showing that you understand how someone *feels*, while active listening demonstrates that you understand what the person is *saying*. These are critical tools for de-escalating emotional conflicts, and the best part is that they cost *nothing* to implement. You do not have to "give up ground" in a conflict to show empathy. Active listening takes a little time, but nothing more. Yet the impact can be substantial.

To dissuade anyone from thinking that these skills are "too fluffy" to merit serious discussion, I first want to share an example of how empathy and active listening were deployed at scale not only to resolve conflicts but to generate millions of dollars in profit.

When I oversaw operations at a technology company, our most popular offering was a subscription to our digital product. If customers forgot to cancel their subscription or simply did not like the service, they would typically contact our customer service team to request a refund. In some cases, these calls could get heated, especially if they were disputing many months of charges.

For a time, our refund policy was simple: if they asked for a refund, give them a refund. In the parlance of the TKI, you might say that our business adopted an "accommodating" style. We did so because it seemed like a customer-friendly policy—and we were quite proud of it.

Then, at the suggestion of our customer service leader, we tested a new approach. On these customer service calls, rather than simply pull the refund lever immediately and end the conflict, we trained our customer service representatives to employ empathy and active listening to engage the customer about what happened and see where the conversation took them. Over the twelve months, our refund rates were cut in half, generating seven-figure savings for the company, which was far more money than the combined salaries of the entire customer service team at that time. And the kicker: customer satisfaction went *up* during the same period. This means we paid out less in refunds and had *happier* customers for it.

Why this win-win? Because through empathy and active listening, our agents were able to move past the superficial problem—a customer wants a refund—and expose deeper issues that they could address without a refund. For example, an agent might learn that a customer wanted a refund because of trouble with the service itself; that agent might talk through the concern, educate the customer, and win the customer back. Or a customer might have been confused about the billing process and want more information. It turned out that customers often had a need that went deeper than simply wanting a few more dollars in their pockets, and finding a genuine, helpful partner on the other end of the phone radically changed the path of those conversations. If a customer still needed a refund, a refund would be provided, but even then, customers appreciated that the person spoke to them like a human being, not a robot, giving them a better overall impression of the company. Everyone was happier.

Employing Empathy

Our agents did not make this transformation overnight; we had to *teach* them how to employ empathy. This may sound pedantic, but it is not; empathy has to be genuine, and people can smell inauthenticity a mile away. How often have you heard customer service agents tell you—in a tone that clearly indicates they are reading from a script—that they are "sorry to hear" about your frustration and are "happy to help" with your problem? These words are so overused that they sound hollow. Colleagues frequently make this same mistake with one another, offering patronizing attempts at empathy that lack sincerity. A failed attempt at empathy does more harm than good.

To overcome these eye-rolling moments, we trained our customer service representatives to dig deeper—to *actually* think about what it would be like to be in the customer's shoes and make that connection. This is the key to empathy, and it's not easy to do when it's the fifth time you have heard the same complaint in one day. Our agents practiced blocking out distractions and focusing on *this* customer and *this* phone call, talking to the person like they would a real friend with a problem. No scripts allowed.

Attorneys need to adopt this same mindset in conflicts with a colleague. Ignore whether you think someone's feelings are justified or not. You cannot dispute how someone feels. Instead, acknowledge the emotion and recognize that you would not want to feel that way either. For example, if a colleague felt betrayed that you picked someone else for a big assignment, focus on how painful it must be for that person to feel a sense of betrayal—not on how the person misunderstood your decision or intentions. Don't say, "I'm sorry you feel that way." Instead, try, "I'm so sorry. I can see how hurt you are, and I feel terrible. I totally understand why that would upset you."

Once you say this, stop talking. Do not add, "But let me explain." We're not ready for explanations yet. Empathy is not a segue. Empathy is a resting place. If you try to move to the next stage too quickly, you will destroy the fragile trust you were just starting to rebuild. Be patient.

These skills do not always come easily to lawyers. When people are trained to be highly analytical—as we all were in law school—it can be difficult to switch gears between problem-solving and empathy. I see this when teaching law students. In my course on professional responsibility (i.e., legal ethics), I always pick one student to role-play a difficult conversation modeled on a real legal case from the 1970s known as the Buried Bodies Case.* This high-stakes, emotional exercise is the perfect test for empathy.

In the exercise, one of my students plays an attorney representing an accused serial killer. The father of one of the suspected victims comes to the attorney's office asking if the attorney has information about his missing daughter. The attorney knows but—because of attorney-client privilege—cannot reveal that the daughter is already dead. I play the distraught father, and although I am no Oscar-winning actor, I do my best to inject real emotions into the scene as I beg and plead with my student (playing the defense attorney) for information about my daughter's whereabouts.

Despite my emotional outpouring and my insistence that they treat the situation as realistically as possible, I have never had a student handle me—the distraught father—with empathy. Instead,

---

* This case is a common staple in professional responsibility courses. It tracks the events surrounding the murders by Robert Garrow in upstate New York. Garrow was represented by Frank Armani and Francis Belge, who kept information about the victims' locations secret in accordance with their ethical responsibilities and faced public backlash when their knowledge came to light. See Lisa G. Lerman and Philip G. Schrag, *Ethical Problems in the Practice of Law*, 4th ed. (Philadelphia: Wolters Kluwer, 2016), 158–73.

they invariably turn matter-of-fact—even cold—telling me they cannot help me, sometimes even reading the ethics rules on confidentiality, as though ABA Model Rule 1.6 would bring me comfort.

Just once, I'd love to see students instead start with, "I am so sorry your daughter is missing. That must be unimaginably difficult." From there, they could let me vent my frustrations while they simply listened. Then, when the time is right, they could explain why they cannot help me. As I tell my students after our dramatic reenactment, you do not have to *decide* between upholding confidentiality and empathy; you can do *both*. This is what I mean when I say that empathy costs nothing. With a more empathetic approach, the distraught father might still leave without the information he seeks, but he might at least leave feeling like he was treated as a human being and not dismissed as collateral damage.

Active Listening

Our second tool for emotional conflicts, active listening, pairs perfectly with empathy. Active listening is largely a fancy way of saying "ask more questions." By asking more questions, you keep people talking, allowing them to express whatever is top of mind. And instead of jumping to problem-solving mode, you can show you listened by summarizing what you heard or paraphrasing the key points back to them to make sure you understand. Again, this must not sound scripted; it should be just as natural as if you were talking to the person at a happy hour and hearing the story for the first time. That kind of authentic conversation between two people is how it should feel *anytime* you are listening to a colleague's concerns.

Active listening is impactful because it satisfies a person's deeper interest in *being heard*. If you meet that need, people are often willing to accept an outcome they might have otherwise found objectionable. This seemingly small kindness can be the key to avoid a conflict turning destructive.

Active listening also builds trust. Salespeople know this precept well, which is why the best salespeople do the *least* talking, instead focusing their energy on asking questions that get the other person talking. Conflicts work the same way. Empathy and active listening build emotional credibility, demonstrating an interest in the *person*, not just the facts. From hostage negotiations to international diplomacy, these lessons are critical.

Empathy and active listening both require practice. But more importantly, they require patience. If you use empathy and active listening to build an emotional connection instead of *dodging* the other person's emotions, you will be far more effective in navigating emotional conflicts.

Attorneys are outstanding problem-solvers, if not by nature then through years of education and experience untangling intellectual knots. But in conflicts with colleagues, overreliance on this intellectual superpower can backfire. Rather than avoiding emotional situations, we have to be ready to address those emotions head-on, whether that means taking better inventory of our own triggers or approaching an emotional colleague with empathy and active listening.

Counterintuitive as it may seem, by holding off on trying to solve "the problem"—that is, by momentarily ignoring the substantive issue of the conflict—and instead following the emotional trail, we may end up discovering that the initial issue that sparked the conflict was only a symptom of a larger problem. Emotions often point us toward the deeper need that is going unmet and causing the colleague's stress, which may be as simple as the basic, human need to be *heard*. In some cases, that is all that's needed to right the ship.

But of course, there will also be times when these tools are not enough. Because while it is *necessary* to approach emotional conflicts with emotional intelligence, that may not be sufficient to neutralize the issue. Even calm, rational beings still have conflicts that turn into logjams, and if we are unable to find a solution, all that work clearing the emotional hazards will be for naught. In the next chapter, we will learn techniques for addressing these stalemates.

CHAPTER 12

BREAKING STALEMATES

When two people want the same thing, and neither will budge, the conflict can seem impenetrable. Yet for world-class negotiators, it is just another day at the office. This chapter will explain how the tools of modern negotiation can make a lawyer more effective in managing conflicts on their teams as well as with opposing counsel or clients.

I will not try to cram my entire negotiation course into a single chapter, particularly because such courses typically involve practical exercises that help build muscle memory, something we cannot do within the pages of a book. Instead, we will zero in on five key techniques that negotiators use to break stalemates and explain how each can be used to ensure conflicts are resolved productively.

But first, we need a bit of setup. The Hollywood vision of negotiators banging on the table and shouting across from each other may be entertaining, but it is not how deals get done. In my classes, we spend considerable time talking about how negotiators have to reframe a conflict not as a fight but as a collaboration. This collaborative model of negotiation is not some ivory-tower, academic framework: it is a critical shift in mindset that opens up new territory for conflict resolution in any setting, including legal teams.

THE ORANGE STORY

The collaborative model of negotiation is best explained through the Orange Story, a classic negotiation fable.

Imagine two chefs at a restaurant—one who makes the entrees and one who makes the desserts. Just before the kitchen closes, the owner comes racing in to tell them that a famous celebrity has just sat down for dinner. Eager to impress the celebrity, both chefs leap into action, gathering the ingredients they need to make their signature dishes. But just as they throw open the doors to the pantry, they both reach in and clap a hand on the very last orange.

That orange is a key ingredient for both dishes; both chefs need it. But there is only one left. What will they do?

After bickering for a few minutes, they do the only logical thing they can think of: they cut the orange in half. The entree chef then takes her half of the orange back to her side of the kitchen and thinks to herself, "Well, it's not enough, but it'll have to do." She then squeezes as much juice as she can from her half of the orange to make a glaze for her steak. Meanwhile, the pastry chef takes his half of the orange back with him, and although he too knows it's not enough, he zests his half of the orange to create icing for his signature cake.

Did you spot their mistake?

Each chef needed a different part of the orange—one needed the juice and one the zest from the peel—so splitting the orange was a foolish solution. If they had only explained *why* they each needed the orange, they could have found a "win-win" solution.

In negotiation parlance, we would say the chefs made the mistake of engaging in *positional bargaining*. Each chef had a position—"I need the orange"—and since they did not think beyond their positions, splitting the orange seemed like the only viable solution. If they had instead focused on *interests*—that is, the "why" behind their positions—they could have found a more creative solution that met all their interests. Shifting from positional bargaining to interest-based bargaining is a key tenet of the collaborative negotiation model.

Not all problems have such neat and tidy solutions, but great negotiators distinguish themselves by looking at a problem—and potential solutions—with more curiosity and more creativity than others. This is what enables them to unlock value that others miss.

Anyone trying to build a high-performance team can benefit from this same way of thinking. Too often, conflicts become deadlocks because team members only take notice of their opposing positions. As a result, they see only a zero-sum game. For me to win, you have to lose. This is sometimes called the competitive model of negotiation. I call this mad grab for value the "Hungry Hungry Hippos" approach.*

---

* For those unfamiliar with this classic children's board game, players slam their hands down on a lever, causing a plastic hippo to dart out and "eat" marbles in the middle of the board. The person who collects the most marbles wins: a classic win-lose proposition.

The collaborative model of negotiation instead reframes the conflict not as a battle between opponents but as a problem-solving exercise between two collaborators working together, united on a single problem: how do we find an agreement that maximizes everyone's interests? They mentally imagine sitting side-by-side with their counterpart, working to unlock this puzzle.

This word "collaborative" may sound familiar. In Chapter 11, we talked about the "collaborative" conflict style, one of five conflict modes in the TKI. In this chapter, we are using the same terms in a separate context—negotiation theory—which can be confusing. Although the words are the same, the nuances and implications are different. There is no ideal TKI mode; all modes have pros and cons depending on the situation, and your mode reflects your most natural style. But in the context of negotiation strategy, most academics teach the "collaborative" (also known as the "principled") negotiation method. We do not teach this method because it sounds nice and friendly; it is the prevailing approach because it generates the best *outcomes*, especially in situations where the parties will have to work together again in the future.[21] That is the situation facing most attorneys.

Similarly, in conflicts with your team members, collaborative approaches can help you find an outcome that satisfies everyone's interests—including your own—without damaging relationships. At first, that might have seemed fanciful, but the Orange Story is a perfect example of a potential win-win solution. By trying to find a solution that works for *both* sides, one might find creative solutions that leave everyone better off.

Of course, just because *you* view the conflict as a collaboration does not mean your counterpart sees it the same way. If that were the case, conflicts would be much simpler. Experts at conflict resolution know how to drag even the most uncooperative individuals into a collaborative conversation—whether they know it or not—by recognizing, and avoiding, positional bargaining.

TECHNIQUE #1: FOCUS ON INTERESTS, NOT POSITIONS

This brings us to our first and most fundamental tool for breaking stalemates on your team. The most common form of stalemate occurs when two people are engaged in positional bargaining. If they have the same position, like our chefs wanting the same orange, they immediately find themselves stuck.

You can break such logjams by pivoting the conversation from positions to interests with one simple question: "Why is _____ important to you?"

The "why" question is critical in negotiations. Some trial lawyers joke that if you ever doze off in trial and wake up not knowing what's going on, your best bet is to shout, "Objection!" I like to say that when a negotiator falls asleep, the thing to do upon waking up is to ask, "Why?" This question virtually always helps move the ball forward.

Asking *why* invites someone to explain the underlying interests behind their demand, revealing information you can use to find more creative solutions. It may seem like a small thing, but it is powerful.

Consider an example where two litigators are trying to decide who will take the lead on an oral argument in an upcoming hearing. Each wants the opportunity, and they have to resolve the issue by themselves. They can't "split" this orange; one person will get to speak in court, and the other will not.

Sounds like a zero-sum game, right? If you were in this situation, you might even think that it would be pointless to ask, "Why is handling this oral argument important to you?" You might think you already know your colleague's answer.

But it would be wrong to make that assumption. People may want the same thing for entirely different reasons. For example, imagine that one attorney has been told in her review to seek out more opportunities to stand up in court. Her next review is just three months away, and she is eager to show progress. The other litigator wants the experience for a slightly different reason; the attorney is newer to the case team and only joined to build a closer relationship with the lead partner. The oral argument will come with extensive mooting with the partner, helping develop that relationship.

If they share these deeper *interests*, rather than getting stuck on their *positions* of wanting the oral argument, they might find a more creative solution. Perhaps the first attorney will take the hearing, since she has a more urgent need to satisfy before her annual review, but she will let the second attorney take over her work on another complex motion that will require close collaboration with the partner. Until we know the true reasons behind someone's positions, we should not assume we are looking at a zero-sum game; a win-win should still be our goal.

Asking "why" can be an iterative process, like peeling back layers of an onion. For example, consider those chefs from earlier. Let's say that the entree chef—who needed the juice of the orange for a glaze—wisely asked the pastry chef why he needed the orange. But now imagine that *both* chefs needed the orange for the same reason: to juice it for their signature recipes. What now?

The answer: ask why again. For example, one might ask the other, "Why is *that recipe* important to you?" Or even, "Why is *cooking for this celebrity* important to you?" These questions might reveal deeper, differing interests. Our goal is to find other interests at play that we can satisfy. For example, maybe one chef's true goal is to meet the celebrity personally and get an autograph, so she ends up changing to another recipe in exchange for the opportunity to bring the dishes out to the celebrity herself.

The point is that none of these potential solutions come to light unless you stop focusing on the initial positions and instead ask about everyone's underlying interests. That is what turns a conflict that feels like a zero-sum game into a richer, more malleable situation. When you ask *why*, more information comes to light that can ultimately break the deadlock.

Not all stalemates will be resolved this way. Perhaps the parties will not be able to identify interests that they can realistically address, even with all of their creative thinking. Or perhaps opposing positions are not the cause of the stalemate. Do not be discouraged; we have only addressed the first of many tools in our toolkit.

TECHNIQUE #2: APPEALING TO COMMON GROUND

Our next technique—appealing to common ground—comes into play when you are in the weeds of a conflict and both sides are arguing based on different facts (or different interpretations of the facts). The classic example is a salary negotiation. Although salary negotiations are not especially common for lawyers at large firms or government agencies where pay is highly regimented, they do occur. And when they do, the conversation can be tense and awkward (to say the least).

Imagine a lawyer who has been serving as deputy general counsel at a private sector company. The lawyer recently learned that other colleagues with the same title at other, larger companies make more money, so he goes to his boss—the general counsel—to ask for higher compensation. This creates a tricky situation for the GC; she wants to retain the deputy, but she believes the pay is fair and does not want to pay more. A conflict ensues as each person—the GC and deputy—points to different sources to justify different compensation figures.

There are many clever ways that the people in this type of negotiation could pursue their interests—salary negotiations are rich fodder for negotiation classes—but many of those tactics are beyond the scope of this book. Instead, our focus is on how we can avoid this conversation between two colleagues from turning into a destructive conflict. Salary negotiations can leave both sides feeling frustrated, and if you are the GC, you do not want one of your high performers feeling undervalued.

Let's assume that the GC employed active listening and empathy (see Chapter 11) to release some of the emotional tension in the negotiation. But the deputy still does not accept that the compensation figure is fair, and at any moment, his anger could boil over if his demands are not met. On the other hand, the GC is confident the salary is appropriate. How should the GC proceed?

Because both attorneys are arguing from different facts, they are like two ships passing in the night. To avoid this stalemate, the GC has to pull out of the weeds and find common ground. Imagine a pyramid of logical arguments, with the disagreement you are currently having at the bottom. Then each layer becomes a bit more abstract as you move up the pyramid. The following graphic is an example.

At the bottom of the salary negotiation conflict, we have two people arguing for different compensation figures. Now go "up" a level by asking yourself *why* each person is offering a different number. Where is that number coming from? Here, each person is using different benchmarks. Now go "up" again: why are these two looking at benchmarks? Because each side thinks benchmarks are relevant to fair pay. And now at the top of the pyramid, we reach a commonality: both sides agree on paying people fairly.

MOVING TO HIGHER GROUND IN A SALARY NEGOTIATION

This is an exercise you conduct in your head, not out loud with the other person. Your goal is to identify that bit of common ground at the top—usually a core principle or value that everyone can support. Then pivot the conversation to that common ground, use it to build trust, and slowly work your way back down the pyramid until you reach a decision.

For example, the GC in our salary conflict might say to the deputy:

Let's take a step back here. At the end of the day, we both want the same thing: we want to make sure that every employee is paid fairly. You work hard and should be compensated appropriately. If we don't pay people fairly, we won't keep them for long. That's what's at stake here. Right?

The GC then pauses to let these words hang in the air a moment. The deputy nods his head in agreement. Notice how the GC is also being open and honest about the concerns at play. This mix of vulnerability and empathy builds trust. Then the GC starts working her way down the pyramid:

The next question for us to answer is *how* to determine what is fair. Not just for your role, either; we need a fair and consistent approach that works for everyone at the company. That's why we're both talking about benchmarks, right? Benchmarks help us confirm that our pay is fair.

Hopefully, more nodding from the deputy. Notice how the GC is starting to plant seeds for her side when she flags the importance of a "consistent approach that works for everyone at the company." If she had highlighted this principle earlier in the conflict—before appealing to common ground—the deputy might have scoffed, thinking the language was just self-serving "corporate speak." But because the GC built trust by finding common ground—salary fairness—the GC's subsequent comments come from a more reasonable place. The GC is building momentum based on trust, rather than fighting an uphill battle.

From there, you can imagine where the conversation might go next. The GC might explain that finding the "right" benchmarks can be difficult because every role at every company is a little different, even if the titles are the same. The GC might also explain the company's process for benchmarking to show transparency. The GC could simply end the conversation there—on a high note—offering to review the deputy's benchmarks with the HR team and come back with a decision. Even if that decision is ultimately unfavorable to the deputy, the GC may have avoided serious damage to the relationship by shifting the conversation from a divisive battle in the weeds to common ground.

TECHNIQUE #3: SEPARATING PRINCIPLES FROM PRAGMATISM

The third technique comes into play in a special class of conflicts marked by these six dreaded words: "It's the principle of the thing!"

These words are a sure sign of a stalemate. They usually indicate that one person is concerned about the larger ramifications of the decision the team faces at the moment, such as setting a "dangerous precedent" or a "slippery slope" for what's to come. We'll call this person the "principlist." On the other side is generally the "pragmatist," someone more concerned with addressing the *present* situation, here and now, even if that means making an exception to the rules.

For example, imagine a deal team that sets an internal policy whereby vacations need to be cleared at least two weeks out so that the team has ample time to plan for coverage. Then one attorney, Tia, requests an exception: she just learned that her parents are coming into town tomorrow, and she wants to take two days off to show them the city. She points out that there are no major deal milestones this week, so the practical impact should not be too severe. But another team member, Brian, balks. "I don't want to ruin your parents' visit," he says. "But it's the principle of the thing. I know other team members have wanted to take brief, spur-of-the-moment trips but didn't even bother asking because of our team policy. We need to be consistent."

This conflict can easily lead to a deadlock because they are *both* right. In an ideal world, we would love to have a policy that is 100% consistent, but we would also like to make case-by-case decisions. We could try to reconcile these approaches—i.e., a broad rule plus guidelines for exceptional situations—but we'll never get it exactly right, and besides, the team needs a PTO policy, not a PTO treatise.

Similarly, consider a situation where a practice group scheduled an important internal training session weeks in advance, and participation is mandatory. Then, the day before the training, a senior associate tells the training leader she cannot attend because of a client call at the same time. The training leader is frustrated, pointing out that skipping the training sends a message to the other, more junior associates that trainings are not important. He asks, "Was this the only time the client could meet?"

"It's not for me to ask the client to work around our training schedule," the associate responds. "The client's needs have to come first."

Here, *both* sides are standing on principle—another potential stalemate. The trainer sees broader consequences for allowing the person to skip the training, and the associate believes that clients should be the top priority. Just as in the first scenario, both sides have a reasonable point. This is why conflicts that involve "principles" can be so challenging to unpack. As lawyers, we tend to appreciate rules, especially rules created for a good reason, and we are quick to point out how exceptions can lead to a slippery slope.

If you find yourself in one of these conflicts, the first step is to acknowledge that *both sides are right*. This can be particularly difficult if you are the one taking the principled stand, because it may feel like you are giving up your principle. That is not the case; you are merely acknowledging that there is a kernel of truth in both arguments. This also means acknowledging that—as a practical matter—there is unlikely to be a perfect answer; some undesirable consequences may be unavoidable. A negotiator calls this risk out early, softening the ground for compromise without explicitly saying *who* will have to give up ground. This is a small nuance, but an effective one in making clear that both sides are equal partners in this challenge. All of these actions help ease the tension and avoid damaging the relationship.

Remember, the decision alone is not what threatens the relationship; it is the journey along the way that tends to cause long-term damage. For example, if the senior associate and the training leader in our last example each dismissed the other's arguments with an eye roll, this otherwise mundane disagreement might turn caustic, with lasting resentment on both sides. Conflict resolution is the art of *de-escalation*.

As for how to resolve the conflict itself, typically, there are two options. The first is to escalate the issue to a neutral third party— a more senior leader, for example—to make a final decision. (More on this approach, known as "changing the players," is coming in Technique #5.) The second option is to try and bifurcate the conflict into two issues and handle each separately: (a) the immediate, practical matter before us today; and (b) how to minimize the long-term consequences of deviating from whatever principle is at stake. That may sound like mental gymnastics, but it's easier to understand with an example.

Return to the scenario with the senior associate planning to skip the mandatory training session. The parties could separate (a) the pressing decision of whether the associate will skip the training or move the client meeting, and (b) the long-term issue of ensuring all associates understand the importance of attending internal programs. By distinguishing these issues, we can unlock creative solutions. For example, the senior associate might indeed skip the session on the condition that she sends an email to the entire practice group apologizing for the scheduling error and acknowledging that attendance at internal trainings remains a top priority. This should help ensure junior associates do not get the wrong idea and think the senior associate's absence is typical.

When someone stands on principle, it rarely makes sense to fight the principle directly. Instead, acknowledge that the principle is a good one, and look for compromises that balance practical concerns and philosophical ones.

TECHNIQUE #4: FOCUS ON A FAIR PROCESS

The importance of a fair process came through in Chapter 9 when debunking the idea that one must choose between the "right" decision and "protecting others' feelings." As we noted, this is a false choice; if people believe the decision-making *process* is fair, they are often willing to accept a decision even if it is not the one they wanted. This principle gives us our fourth conflict resolution tactic: when you have to make a decision that might be unpopular, focus on ensuring a fair process.

Lawyers are all familiar with the concept of *due process*. To paraphrase that centuries-old concept, before rendering judgment against someone, the person should have notice and a chance to be heard. This is a useful framework for resolving conflicts on a team as well.

For example, suppose your law firm is expanding to a new building, which means new seating arrangements for everyone. If you have not had the pleasure of leading an "office shuffle," I can tell you that the one thing law firms, businesses, and government agencies all have in common is that no matter how stable they seem, they are all one "office shuffle" away from a full-blown civil war. It's a bureaucratic powder keg, with everyone having different notions of the "best way" to decide who should sit where. Some want to maximize choice, with lotteries based on rank or tenure. Others want to optimize networks, putting people who work together near each other. Still others want to maximize "employee mixing," intentionally co-locating employees who do not work together to build relationships across groups. Even after the COVID-19 pandemic, when many organizations were returning to the office on a relaxed, hybrid schedule, these debates still cause headaches for organizations.

A conflict of this complexity has no perfect solution. In fact, it's about as close to a "lose-lose" situation as one can get: from the decision-maker's perspective, the sheer number of parties and moving parts virtually guarantees that most people will have some unmet complaint about the outcome. And when that anger is channeled toward the leadership team, it can seriously undermine their credibility (and become a gossip-fueling distraction).

When faced with such a challenge, many leaders go into a room, lock the door, and do not come out until a decision is reached. This reminds me of the papal conclave, where the College of Cardinals meets in total secrecy to decide the next pope, sparking speculation and drama until the famous white smoke appears. Decisions on legal teams should not be this dramatic. Yet leaders routinely choose this opaque route because they do not see any point in opening the conversation with the team. They fear the debate will get out of hand and consume everyone's time. "We cannot decide everything by committee," many leaders would say.

These concerns are understandable, but is there really no middle ground? Take a moment and think about how you might approach this situation differently if you were in charge.

A better strategy starts with a bit of transparency about the process to come. For example, you might announce that the firm needs to decide new seating arrangements in the next sixty days. Then you might explain that since this is a difficult decision with many trade-offs, you are going to create space for people to share their suggestions and concerns. You could even outline the process as follows:

DESCRIPTION	DEADLINE
Phase 1: Everyone will have access to an online survey where they are free to send suggestions about how they believe seating should be determined.	Day 15
Phase 2: Leadership will review the input and come up with a draft seating arrangement.	Day 30
Phase 3: Everyone will have access to the draft seating arrangement and be able to submit a new round of feedback with questions or concerns (another online survey).	Day 45
Phase 4: Leadership will publish the final seating chart.	Day 60

Before you scoff at this four-phase approach as overkill, consider this: nothing stops the leaders from making their own decision. After all, leaders are not promising to accommodate everyone's suggestions; the only commitment they are making is to listen. If they find the input valuable, which they likely will, they might alter their decision; if not, they will stick to their guns.

I am not suggesting that leaders should disingenuously seek input that they have every intention of ignoring. I am simply pointing out that creating space for people to share input does not bind leaders' hands. Nor does it require a significant amount of time and energy; creating an online questionnaire is a five-minute exercise for anyone who has used Google Forms or similar tools. Moreover, the feedback that leaders receive through a more open process can be genuinely useful and productive.

Leaders sometimes object to this approach because they fear opening Pandora's Box. They worry it will invite chaos at the office, with comments and proposals flying around like hotcakes, distracting everyone from their day jobs.

Quite the opposite. If a subject is controversial, you cannot stop people from forming opinions, much less stop them from sharing those opinions with their colleagues. If you do nothing, you simply force this gossip underground, where it causes more harm and distraction. By providing a process for collecting input, you channel that energy. And by inviting team members into the process as collaborators, you avoid a dynamic where they feel this decision is happening "to" them.

The technique of focusing on a fair process is useful not just in complex, system-wide changes like reseating an office, but *anytime* a leader may have to make an unpopular decision. And creating a fair process need not always be so elaborate. For example, imagine a partner is publishing an article with the help of several associates, and the partner must decide which names will appear as official authors. Partners sometimes make this decision in private, with the associates only learning that their names were not included when the article went to print. This kind of conflict avoidance can feel like a stab in the back, undermining trust and creating deeper rifts within the team.

Instead, the partner might draft a few sentences explaining how other partners have typically handled co-author credit in the past, share it with associates, and ask if they have any feedback. The associates may not actually share any feedback, but the gesture demonstrates that everyone has an *opportunity* to be heard, even on controversial issues. Transparent processes like this encourage productive conflicts, rather than destructive ones.

Because this technique is so important—and so often overlooked—let's talk through one final example of a type of conflict that is far less dramatic but nevertheless frustrating for team members: a disagreement over strategy. This can happen in litigation, transactional matters, and even client pitches, where attorneys have different ideas for the best path forward. These discussions usually start out calm and rational, but because attorneys can be quite attached to their own ideas—especially if they assume an ownership mindset—these disagreements can become heated.

If you find yourself in the position of decision-maker for one of these tense battles, you can use the notion of fair process to make your ultimate decision more palatable. The best part is that, in this case, the execution is simple—no "multi-phase plan" needed. Explain to the team members that you are not sure of the best course and want to hear one last time from all perspectives. Go around the table (or videoconference) and give everyone a fixed amount of time—e.g., ninety seconds—to provide their final thoughts. Then tell them you want to take some time to think about it overnight before making a final decision.

By giving everyone a chance to be heard and taking a break to digest, you send a signal that you value everyone's perspective enough to ruminate on their suggestions fully. When you announce your decision, the team will be more likely to accept the outcome, no matter which side each team member was on originally.

Hopefully, these examples demonstrate how leaders can make difficult, even unpopular decisions—both large and small—without leaving a path of destruction in their wake.

TECHNIQUE #5: DEFUSING HARDBALL TACTICS

Our final technique centers on hardball tactics, where one person in the conflict resorts to more aggressive or manipulative behavior. This could include making rude comments, stubbornness (formally known as "refusing to negotiate"), as well as pressure tactics like threatening to quit or to call the person's boss.

In my negotiation class, we devote two full weeks to this topic (and could do much more). The truth is, while these tense situations seem intimidating at first, with a bit of training, anyone can learn to navigate them effectively.

Since this is not a negotiation book, we will only scratch the surface of hardball tactics. Our goal, after all, is to learn how to manage workplace conflicts, and thankfully, the kinds of hardball tactics that occasionally fly between aggressive opponents in a negotiation are not as common among peers on a legal team.

But when these tactics do occur, they can cause irreparable damage, so having a basic understanding of how to manage these situations can better equip you to contain the fallout.

The key principle to keep in mind is that your goal is to *defuse* the hardball tactics, not *destroy* the other person. For example, if someone makes a condescending comment, you may be tempted to hit right back—perhaps even harder. But if you hope to resolve the conflict peacefully, you will need to avoid these emotionally satisfying but ultimately unproductive moves. They only exacerbate the conflict and drive your counterpart to fight harder.

Instead, look for a way to build the person a *bridge* back to the collaborative side of the conflict. Let's start with someone who makes a snide remark. Assuming you are able to maintain your own emotions—no easy task, as we discussed in Chapter 11—you might then say to the person, "Comments like that aren't helping us solve the problem. I know you don't mean anything by it; you're just upset. I'm frustrated too. Let's take a break and regroup in a bit."

The same principle applies to handling pressure tactics. Suppose a partner threatens to quit if the head of the firm does not support an aggressive expansion plan. The head of the firm might respond to this threat by acknowledging the threat as a legitimate option—not dismissing it—and then pivoting to other options. For example, the head of the firm might say:

I agree that one way of resolving this conflict is to part ways. I hope it doesn't come to that, but it is our last resort. Before that happens, let's make sure we exhaust all other options first, including your hiring proposal. Can you walk me through...

Essentially, the head of the firm is responding to the threat as though it were just another "option" under consideration. This takes the punch out of the threat and allows for a clean segue back to the *other* option—deciding on an agreeable hiring plan. If the head of the firm can get the frustrated partner back to talking about the proposal, that is already a productive step in the right direction. As the saying goes: if we're talking, we're negotiating. This is how one can turn a stubborn opponent into a collaborator.

Whatever language you use, make sure you give the person a way to return to the table and abandon these hardball tactics *without* having to admit the tactics failed. In other words, you have to allow an opportunity to *save face*. People want to maintain their dignity, especially if they are losing an argument. If you are successful in creating this bridge, your counterpart will leave the hardball tactics behind, allowing you to get the conflict back on a productive track.

None of this is intended to suggest that leaders should allow a colleague to freely engage in destructive hardball tactics. These tactics can be offensive (and potentially unethical). Managers have a responsibility to give people feedback and, where appropriate, take disciplinary action when team members behave irresponsibly. But there will be times when it pays to know how to handle these difficult situations pragmatically. I have watched senior attorneys who worked together for many years spiral into animosity after one late-night argument took a harsh turn. In these tense moments, the right words at the right time can make all the difference in avoiding permanent damage.

If you cannot break the cycle of hardball tactics, consider letting someone else have a turn—a technique known as "changing the players." That person could be another peer—essentially a second opinion—or a superior. For example, you might say, "It seems like we're not making progress. Maybe I'm missing something here. Why don't we see if Lynn has a different way to think about the problem?" You might be surprised how often an angry colleague turns into a thoughtful collaborator the instant someone new enters the discussion.

One piece of advice for more junior team members: do not make the mistake of thinking that if you are watching a conflict unfold between more senior team members, you have no role to play. As a neutral observer, you may have a unique opportunity to be the voice of reason that both sides need to hear to jolt them out of their belligerence. If you are able to interject safely, your words can help de-escalate the situation and give everyone a chance to come back from the brink.

Every single team member has a role to play in preserving a culture of productive conflict. Whether you are a first-year associate or a senior leader at the organization, you can do your part to support the team. Remember, this is *your* team; team harmony is in *your* best interest. If you own your role in conflicts—even conflicts you did not start—you can become a powerful force for change and inspiration in your organization.

PUTTING IT ALL TOGETHER

By reframing each conflict as a problem we can work together to solve—a true collaboration—we can find ways to break stalemates and avoid lasting animosity on our teams. This mindset helps ensure that conflicts do not destroy all the work we have done to encourage trust and establish an ownership mentality.

We covered a lot of ground in this single chapter. Before we move on, below is a summary of the five techniques for managing obstacles and breaking stalemates in conflicts. (You can download a digital version at *allrisebook.com*.)

TECHNIQUE	WHEN TO USE	HOW TO USE
Focus on Interests (Not Positions)	When we both want, but cannot both have, the same thing (i.e., a zero-sum game)	Ask, "Why is _____ important to you?" Then look for creative solutions.
Appeal to Common Ground	When both sides are arguing from different facts and perspectives	Move higher up in the interests pyramid. Talk about broader goals or principles you can agree on, then work your way back down.
Separate Principles and Pragmatism	When either of you says "it's the principle of the thing" or warns of a "slippery slope"	Acknowledge that both sides are right. Escalate to a third party or bifurcate the present decision from any "downstream consequences" and address the issues separately.
Focus on Fair Process	When you are a manager who may have to make an unpopular decision	Explain your decision-making process and ensure everyone is heard before making a call.
Defuse Hardball Tactics	When someone engages in manipulative behavior or pressure tactics	Build the person a bridge back to the collaborative side of the conflict. Leave them a way to save face or they may dig themselves deeper. As a last resort, consider bringing in someone new to offer a fresh perspective ("changing the players").

Of course, one chapter on negotiation does not do the subject justice. For more information, consider the negotiation classic *Getting to Yes* by the famous Roger Fisher, William Ury, and Bruce Patton,[22] as well as William Ury's follow-up, *Getting Past No*,[23] which focuses on breaking through the toughest negotiation barriers. The more recent book *Never Split the Difference* by Chris Voss[24] offers additional techniques and specific tips on

language for tricky conflicts. To parrot my students at the end of
a semester, the investment you make in becoming a better negotiator will pay dividends in all manner of conflicts—both in and
outside of work.

———————

As we end this final chapter on conflicts, remember that at the
most fundamental level, conflicts are a *good* thing for our teams.
They bring out our best ideas and generate the kind of contagious,
positive energy that makes us proud to work with our colleagues.
But for lawyers accustomed to an adversarial process, you have
to be careful to keep conflicts from turning destructive. If you
can help your teams maintain this balance, then you have all the
ingredients needed to reach our final trait of high-performance
teams: accountability.

PART 4

ACCOUNTABILITY

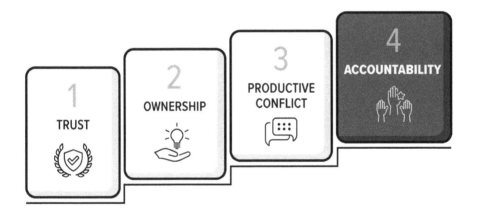

CHAPTER 13

GOING SUPERSONIC

On the morning of October 14, 1947, Chuck Yeager piloted the experimental X-1 airplane to Mach 1.07, bringing an end to the U.S. military's battle against the sound barrier. This first-ever supersonic flight required extraordinary feats of engineering. Many people believed that pushing a plane beyond the sound barrier would inevitably cause it to break apart, a theory buttressed by the fact that several test pilots lost their lives in their attempts.

To reach such a demanding level of power and performance without losing stability, the engineers had to consider every aspect of the plane's design: a new shape for the fuselage, thinner wings, a first-of-its-kind moving tailplane, and more. The plane could not even take off on its own; it had to be attached to a larger plane, a B-29, and then "launched" by disconnecting the X-1 midair at 20,000 feet. This was because the X-1 needed every ounce of fuel onboard for its supersonic acceleration; it could not waste precious rocket fuel on such trivialities as takeoff. (Or landing, for that matter. It had to glide back to the runway after the flight was complete.)[25]

These tweaks—and hundreds more—made all the difference. Instead of the plane ripping apart as it crossed the sound barrier, the trip was "smooth as a baby's bottom," Yeager would later write. "Grandma could be sitting up there sipping lemonade."[26] That is what the ultimate echelon of performance feels like.

On our teams, we want much the same thing: maximum performance—even under high pressure—without ripping the team apart. But one does not reach this level of efficiency overnight. Nor does a single leader drive the team to peak performance through sheer force of will like some kind of shrewdly ingenious dictator.

Instead, teams reach their fullest potential only by pushing *each other* to achieve great things. That is the power of *accountability*.

Accountability reflects team members' willingness to hold each other—and themselves—to high standards. When team members push each other, every individual becomes both a player and a coach at the same time. This magnifies the impact of each person's contributions.

This higher gear of performance does not mean everyone has to sacrifice all other priorities outside of work. Nor does accountability mean managers must become "enforcers" of quality, creating a culture of fear. Quite the opposite. If we squeeze teams too tightly, they will crumble under the pressure or burn out trying. Burnout is not just bad for morale; it's bad for business, draining profits as attorneys' time and the organization's money are spent recruiting and training replacement team members.

Ideally, true accountability does not come "top-down" but rather from within, like a social contract *between* team members. That is, everyone should agree and commit to certain standards because everyone *wants* the team to produce the best work possible—not because the boss says so. If this commitment is genuine, the virtuous cycle can begin.

Teams that have this special quality are inspiring. In college, I joined our school's fledgling mock trial team as a way of testing the waters of my interest in the law. I found a group of charismatic, intelligent, and thoughtful individuals, and together we comprised a truly *mediocre* mock trial team. Despite our best intentions, our performance was cringeworthy. (And I have the video clips to prove it.)

But the following year, something strange happened. As one of my teammates would later say, "We just sort of decided that we wanted to start winning, and then we put in an ungodly amount of work to make it happen." We spent countless late nights writing and practicing for our trials. We would record our examinations and arguments, replay them, and critique them down to the most granular details in front of the entire team. And just to be clear: this was in *college*. We had no illusions that anyone would care about "collegiate mock trial" on our resumes in the long run; we just felt we had something special on our team and wanted to see what we could do.

It took two years, but we reached our goal of winning the national championship. There was no fame or cash prize for our trouble. Just a large, plastic trophy—one that we dropped and broke within two hours. But none of that mattered. All that mattered to us was building the best team we could. It was an end unto itself.

The point of this trip down memory lane is simply that special things happen when team members rally together to set high standards on their own. That intrinsic accountability—as opposed to accountability that comes from management on high—makes hard work more rewarding. This is what allows teams to reach a higher gear than they otherwise thought possible.

Accountability also bestows an incredible level of efficiency. Accountable team members require less hand-holding. They learn faster. They complete their work on time and with fewer revisions. Late nights and weekend work still occur, but not as often, and more as a release valve than an inevitability. Everything just seems to "come together" in an unforgettable way.

On the other hand, when a team lacks accountability, the symptoms can be just as memorable. One of my consulting clients was chock full of talented individuals with extraordinary experience and dedication to their work. They trusted each other, had genuine ownership, and embraced conflict. But despite these qualities, progress always felt like a *slog*. Projects routinely took more time and energy than expected. Ambiguous timelines and vague action items routinely led to confusion and last-minute scrambling. Team leaders had to pull the team over the finish line personally, often working late to fill in gaps and correct mistakes. And because the work did not always meet their high bar for quality, managers became gatekeepers, which also meant they became bottlenecks.

These two operational extremes may not mean the difference between life and death, as was the case for Chuck Yeager, but the stakes are still high. Legal teams with true accountability outpace other teams in nearly every respect, not just in the quality of the work but also the overall satisfaction of the team, making for a higher-retention, more profitable organization. A win-win.

Luckily, you do not have to start from scratch to build this culture. In fact, we have already covered many important prerequisites for encouraging accountability.

For example, for team members to hold each other accountable, they must develop *trust* through psychological safety. Without that trust, team members will shy away from giving one another feedback.

Similarly, accountability requires *ownership*. If I do not care about the bigger picture beyond the four corners of my assigned tasks, I will not take the risk of trying to help elevate the team. And Chapter 7 went deeper into ownership for managers, highlighting lessons around the importance of a *teaching mentality* for solving problems on teams without crossing over into micromanagement—a lesson that will come back again and again in this section.

Finally, accountability cannot thrive if team members fear that their suggestions will provoke destructive *conflicts*, which is why, in the last section, we explored the signs of destructive conflicts and learned how to avoid letting those harmful patterns consume our teams.

So here we are: the final leg of our journey for building high-performance legal teams. Over the next few chapters, we will address three key ingredients for unlocking accountability: project management, autonomy, and feedback. Then, in the final chapter, we will turn our attention to a broader type of accountability, with tools for senior leaders to evaluate the progress of teams (and the entire organization) over time.

Together, these tools ensure that all team members understand what is expected, have the space to work, and help each other learn and grow. After a few cycles working together in this way, these teams become exponentially more effective. Through this virtuous cycle of continuous improvement, such teams don't just accelerate; they go supersonic.

CHAPTER 14

PROJECT MANAGEMENT

P roject management may sound like an intuitive—even obvious—set of skills, but try telling that to a product manager at a tech company overseeing software engineers. They do not manage from the hip; they perfect their process over the course of many years. In fact, they experiment with their process constantly, getting feedback and making tweaks so they can improve. Every bit of efficiency they can squeeze out of their team makes for a happier—and more profitable—operation.

On a well-organized legal team, time is never wasted. All attorneys (and nonlegal team members) understand the team's objectives, including how this project fits into the big picture. They understand how their tasks contribute to that objective, allowing them to prioritize their time efficiently. When they meet, they know the purpose of the meeting and do not waste time on tangents or discussing issues relevant only to a subset of the group. In short, everyone knows precisely what is expected of them and of the team as a whole.

This clarity is what allows accountability to thrive. But if attorneys want to run teams this smoothly, they have to set the right expectations.

In this chapter, we will explore several best practices that are common in other industries but often overlooked in the legal field. First, we will walk through tactics for better team meetings. Then we will talk about broader process improvements that can make teams much more efficient.

Most of the examples we will cover relate to client work, but this chapter will address internal projects as well. After all, attorneys routinely participate in (or lead) a wide range of organizational initiatives, from revamping recruitment to social planning to practice group strategy.

BETTER MEETINGS

Attorneys hate wasting their time in meetings. But meetings themselves are not the enemy. The problem is that we use our time in meetings poorly, either because we picked the wrong kind of meeting for the job—yes, there is more than one kind of meeting—or because we do not impose structure within the meeting for dealing with the kinds of time-wasting distractions that drain the team's efficiency (and happiness).

Let's start with the four different types of team meetings, each with their own function: stand-up, tactical, strategic, and—in unique circumstances—offsites. Attorneys often lump these together, which is exactly why meetings go off the rails.

The Stand-Up

A "stand-up" is a short meeting—generally ten to fifteen minutes—where team members give a brief report on their work and any roadblocks they are encountering. These check-ins are useful for monitoring progress and ensuring alignment, which is why case teams and deal teams might have them every week or even every day during busy matters. They are called "stand-ups" because, traditionally, people would physically stand for the entire meeting, a testament to the meeting's brevity. Even over a videoconference, the name (and concept) remain the same.

Because these meetings are so brief, stand-ups are not useful for solving problems. In fact, trying to solve problems live during a stand-up is a cardinal sin of meeting management. (Some teams even make sinners pay a penance, like buying coffee for the team the next morning.) Instead, if someone brings up a problem that requires collaboration to solve, the relevant team members are supposed to schedule a separate meeting—outside the stand-up—to discuss. This avoids wasting the rest of the team's time.

Stand-ups are especially useful for high-pressure, tight-turn-around situations, like deal teams near closing or litigation teams heading to trial. Stand-ups typically happen first thing in the morning to ensure the team is aligned on the day's top priorities. But teams working long hours will often shift stand-ups to occur later in the day, such as 5 p.m., to give team leaders a chance to confirm which tasks require late-night work and which can wait until morning. For teams concerned about burnout, these end-of-day stand-ups can have a significant impact on work-life balance.

A word of warning: avoid the temptation of conducting your fifteen-minute stand-up at the start of your longer (thirty-minute or sixty-minute) weekly team meeting. If you do, you'll find the check-ins take longer and longer until they crowd out the rest of your agenda. Having separate, dedicated time for a stand-up with a hard stop at the end avoids this overflow problem.

The Tactical

Tactical meetings are weekly or bi-weekly team meetings, generally thirty to sixty minutes, for addressing larger issues that affect the entire team. Agendas for team meetings should always be set in advance to avoid "agenda creep," and it helps to time-box the issues with estimates for how long each issue will take. If an issue goes over the allotted time, do not simply let momentum take over; pause the meeting for a quick check-in with the group to decide whether to allow the extra time or move the topic to a separate meeting. This ten-second decision can rescue a meeting from the clutches of a time-sucking black hole.

Lawyers sometimes worry this kind of rigor will come off condescending, but once you have conducted a few meetings this way, you will never go back. People find it incredibly frustrating to be in meetings that seem to veer off in whatever direction pleases the team leader (or the loudest talker). Staying on agenda and having a consistent meeting discipline sets clear expectations that everyone understands—and follows.

One additional nuance for running better meetings: note whether each agenda item is an "inform" or "consult" topic. Inform-only topics are typically announcements that require little or no response except clarifying questions, such as an update from the lead partner about a recent high-level meeting with the client. On the other hand, consultation topics are those where the team's input is welcome. Sort your agenda so that inform-only matters are at the *end* of the agenda; that way, if time runs short, you can push the information out to the team via email instead. This ensures that most of your team meeting is spent on the most impactful, most collaborative issues.

The Strategic Session

The third type of meeting, the strategic session, typically lasts two hours or more and focuses on a single subject that requires more time and space to address. This type of session is useful for topics that simply do not fit within a weekly team meeting. Sometimes, these meetings cover issues of case or deal strategy, such as mapping out the optimal sequence for depositions or war-gaming an M&A negotiation. But I prefer to think of the term "strategic session" as a nod to the fact that a two-hour block of time can itself be a more efficient, more *strategic* use of the team's time than a shorter block.

For example, I have worked with practice groups on implementing changes to their internal processes around everything from tracking PTO to feedback to deal management. Typically, they set up a small team or committee to tackle the problem, and then this team meets in thirty-minute or sixty-minute chunks over several weeks. But context-shifting from case work to committee work is costly; every meeting requires several wasted minutes remembering where the last meeting left off, and momentum is difficult to build. After a month, the team might only have made minimal progress. A more strategic approach to time management would be to have a single, longer session, such as a two-hour meeting, where the team can accomplish far more than they would with two separate one-hour meetings a week or more apart. Lawyers can find it difficult to carve out larger chunks of time like this, but in the end, the improved efficiency actually *saves* time.

Brainstorming is another classic example of a strategic meeting. If your team requires space for creative thinking, trying to squeeze it into an already-packed tactical meeting will not do the exercise justice. Hold a strategic session dedicated to the topic so that you can accomplish more in one "surge" rather than a fragmented discussion.

The Offsite

Private sector companies are accustomed to the concept of offsites—longer sessions, usually over one to three days, that provide the team time to set aside day-to-day work and focus on bigger picture issues. Typically, offsites include work events during the day and social activities in the evening, the combination of which builds stronger professional and personal bonds between team members. Businesses use these sessions to tackle challenges such as long-term strategy, company values, and other weighty matters.

Attorneys need time for these activities as well. Taking two to three days away from client work is understandably challenging, but for attorneys working in-house and even in some practice groups, having this dedicated time together can propel the team forward.

First, for fully remote legal teams, offsites provide a critical opportunity to build those strong team bonds that come with in-person interaction. In the book *Remote: Office Not Required*, the founders of the tech company Basecamp explain how they built their company without ever having physical office space (long before the COVID-19 pandemic), and one of the keys to their success was the thoughtful use of offsites to encourage in-person connections.[27] With just two to four offsites per year, many remote organizations build the bonds they need to sustain them through the long periods without true in-person contact.

Second, for practice groups that already see each other in person regularly, even a single-day session outside the office can offer a much-needed break from the daily rhythm of intense client work and allow teams to connect more deeply. There are several ways to use the time productively, for example:

- Practice group leaders can discuss their long-term strategy, helping associates feel more connected to the "business" side of the firm.
- Breakout sessions can address topics around team culture (e.g., team values, work-life balance, and feedback) or team processes (e.g., project management, retrospectives, and team norms—more on these in a moment).
- The team can also engage in trust-building exercises like those described in Chapter 4, such as talking through differences in Social Styles.

As an offsite draws near, many attorneys will become anxious about taking a full day (or two) away from client work. Short "email breaks" can be included in the agenda to ease the pressure. But regardless of the skepticism some attorneys may express before the session, nearly everyone will become a believer by the end. The dedicated time away from the office naturally brings people together, and if you have a good facilitator for the sessions, they will be incredibly valuable. Consider bringing in someone from your professional development team or an outside facilitator (budget permitting) to ensure you get the most from your time.

Some financially-constrained organizations will not be able to transport attorneys offsite and pay for lodging and other expenses. In those cases, consider hosting an "onsite-offsite," where you clear schedules for the day but use the existing office space and conference rooms to host your sessions. Or, as an in-between option, consider keeping everyone local to avoid travel expenses but renting a conference room at a nearby hotel for a change of scenery. Just be aware that the more distance you can get from the office, the more likely it will be that attorneys can set aside the distractions of their daily work and focus on broader topics.

Offsites do not need to be extravagant, alcohol-laden boondoggles. With a healthy balance of strategic sessions and bonding time, these offsites not only help teams learn how to work better together, but the deeper connections they generate will boost employee morale and employee retention. That's a strong return on investment.

PROCESS IMPROVEMENTS

Better team meetings are only the beginning. Next, every project management toolkit needs the right processes to streamline how team members work together. We will cover a number of tactics in the pages that follow—meeting management tools, task tracking, retros, and team norms—but there is one overriding theme: teams work better when the rules of engagement are clear. If one attorney tries to shoehorn these changes, the impact will be slow. But if team members openly discuss and embrace these improvements, the impact can happen practically overnight. This is how change management works; the group has to understand the change and commit together to maximize the impact. Once expectations are set, people will hold each other *accountable* to these processes, ensuring that they stick.

Meeting Management Tools

In our earlier discussion about regular weekly and biweekly meetings, we noted the importance of agendas in keeping meetings on track. Most attorneys would say that agendas make meetings more efficient, but few actually use them. There is an overall sense that teams that know each other well do not need such "formalities." Big mistake. Agendas are not about bureaucracy; they are tools for aligning priorities. Teams operating without agendas consistently waste a tremendous amount of their time (and thereby, the client's money) in meetings on tangential topics and lower priority issues that did not need the entire group's attention.

We covered several nuances of agendas earlier, such as including time estimates for each topic, starting with "consult" topics and moving "inform" topics to the end, and being intentional about deviating from the agenda rather than letting momentum lead your meeting astray. We won't belabor those points again here except to say that the more rigor, the better.

In addition to agendas, attorneys must be just as attentive to documenting action items at the end of the meeting. Again, I recognize that this sounds obvious, but if you ask people at the end of a meeting to list their action items, you will regularly find discrepancies, misunderstandings, or ambiguities that lead to frustration later. My rule is simple: every action item needs to be documented (*in writing*) with one name and a clear deadline—no exceptions. Every aspect of this rule is important. As you try to write out your action items, you will likely realize details that were ambiguous when discussing it orally. If you put more than one name against an action item—or worse, no name—then the action item will fall between the cracks of responsibility. And finally, if you do not assign a clear date, you cannot be surprised when the task takes longer to complete than you had hoped.

A nuanced tip: for complex action items with multiple parts, document at least the immediate next step with a name and date to ensure it keeps moving. For example, imagine that in your team meeting, the team rallies around the idea of a dedicated training module on e-discovery or some other subject matter. It is probably too early to decide who will deliver the training and when the training will occur, so do not make that your action item. Instead, you might assign someone to "reach out to the professional development team and work with them to draft a timeline for the training." Then for the date field, pick a deadline by which the person will be expected to *report back* to the team with that recommendation. Then repeat this process for each step of the project. These small differences in how you assign action items will help ensure everyone stays on track.

The third tip for better meetings is a bit cheeky but popular among several of my clients. In his book *Traction*, Gino Wickman describes watching team meetings go off the rails so many times that he encourages team members who spot these derailments to shout, "Tangent alert!"[28] I have seen teams adopt this light-hearted way of calling attention to deviations from the agenda, and it becomes a bit of a game—with genuinely useful consequences for better meetings. Small gestures like these democratize meeting management and allow team members to hold each other accountable to their agenda. As always, adapt these ideas to find what fits your culture.

Task Tracking

Thanks to your well-run meetings, you now have a list of action items. Rather than just emailing these out after the meeting, keep your list of action items up-to-date in a central repository—generally known as a "tracker."

The tracker is a shared document accessible to everyone on the team, not just hoarded by the team leader. It should clearly indicate the action item, owner, and deadline at a minimum. Teams will usually add other columns depending on their project, such as a "status" column (on track, off track, complete, or not started—usually color-coded) and space for additional notes. For example, here is a sample tracker for managing a diligence process that includes references to specific document numbers in the deal papers:

DOC	DESCRIPTION	OWNER	DUE	STATUS	ISSUES
A1	Funding notice	Janae	4/1	On Track	None
A2	Conversion notice	Doug	4/3	Off Track	Need guidance on xyz
...	...	...	...	...	...
...	...	...	...	...	...

Make this a live, shared document that everyone can edit (rather than a local file on one person's laptop) so that team members can see assignments and track updates. Better yet, use online apps dedicated to project management, like Notion, Monday, or Asana. Even Excel and Google Docs can be a good choice as long as the documents are shared with the team.*

---

* Attorneys sometimes ask whether the use of these third-party platforms might violate the ethical rules of confidentiality. Since the age of email, there...

If you want more advice on how best to implement these ideas, look no further than your colleagues on the business side of your organization. After one of my training sessions, the firm's director of professional development noted that while attorneys seemed largely unfamiliar with (and often allergic to) these online tools, they are a staple for the rest of the firm—namely, the business and support teams—and for good reason. Once you use the right tool for the job, you never go back. Ask around your organization and see if your colleagues can help you get started.

The second technique for task tracking is the "parking lot." In my consulting days, the parking lot was a euphemism employed anytime someone brought up an idea that we wanted to politely throw in the trash. "Great suggestion, Bob. Let's put that in the parking lot for now and come back to it later"—meaning never. But I now show teams the value of a *real* parking lot—a place to hold onto ideas and suggestions that we are not ready to address today but do not want to lose forever.

For example, imagine that, during a team discussion about how to ensure coverage for a colleague's upcoming vacation, the conversation derails into a back-and-forth about the need for a better way to consolidate everyone's vacation schedules for plan-ning purposes. Instead of just shouting, "Tangent alert!"—and cutting off the conversation—the team could instead record the suggestion on a list in a shared document to come back to later.

This list—the parking lot—is not a place where ideas go to die. Instead, once a quarter, you should review the ideas in the parking

---

...are many ethics opinions supporting the use of third-party platforms for information management so long as the attorney takes reasonable diligence to secure access to the information. But every state is a bit different, so if you have concerns, you should conduct your own research. Your IT team can also be helpful in maintaining proper security.

lot together as a team, looking for anything that ought to be prioritized. If an idea is selected, you then remove it from the parking lot, decide the first step to take, and record that action item in the tracker. Then cull extraneous or duplicative items from the parking lot and sort the remaining items by their importance for next time. This process is called "grooming" (a term used in agile project management to refer to the process of going through the backlog and deciding what to address next).

The parking lot provides teams a balance between staying on agenda and not losing track of spontaneous ideas. It is also a great source of inspiration when trying to decide what "big picture" topics to discuss at a team offsite.

Hopefully, you can see how a well-organized tracker and parking lot can complement each other. The tracker helps with day-to-day action items, while the parking lot preserves ideas that might become action items in the future. Items can be elevated from the parking lot to the tracker, or they can be deprioritized from the tracker and moved down to the parking lot. Everything has its place; nothing is lost. Once everyone understands how to use these tools, they become second nature.

Retros

The next tool for process improvement—the "retro," short for "retrospective"—comes into play after a big milestone. A retro is a meeting where the team gathers to reflect on what went well and what improvements they would make next time.* For example, if

---

* This is also sometimes called a "post-mortem" discussion, though that language tends to cause teams to focus on what went wrong. In a retro, it is important to highlight both positive and constructive lessons.

a litigation team completes a major filing, such as an extensive summary judgment motion, they might schedule thirty minutes for a retro on the drafting process. During this time, they could discuss whether assignments were clear, whether they had the right cadence of stand-ups and tactical meetings, the need for additional training, and so on.

The retro helps highlight opportunities to improve in the future, which is why it is particularly useful on legal teams. I have seen deal teams create multi-page templates to guide their retro conversations so that they get the most out of the discussion, recognizing that every improvement they make is a win. But retros are also useful on internal project teams, such as after launching a new mentorship initiative or even after a few months living with a new PTO policy.

The key is to make these conversations about learning, not judgment. I also recommend storing the results of these retros somewhere that everyone—but most importantly, senior leaders—can see them. This transparency gives those who are less involved in day-to-day work a peek into how the team is functioning. Retros can also help leaders identify knowledge gaps so they can set training priorities.

Team Norms

Our final tactic for process improvement—the setting of team norms—is a bit more abstract than the others. Think of team norms as a collection of social contracts between team members that help set expectations for how they work together. For example, the following list is based on real norms from clients over the years:

- **Email Communication**: Emails should be answered within 24 hours. If you need more time for a substantive response, it is acceptable to say that, so long as you do so within 24 hours and indicate when you plan to deliver a more detailed reply.

- **Nights and Weekends**: If you email a colleague outside the range of 9 a.m. to 8 p.m. on workdays and need a prompt response, you should text or call them to let them know. Otherwise, the colleague may reasonably assume the email can wait until normal working hours.

- **Surface, Don't Solve**: If you come across an unexpected roadblock, such as an ambiguous issue in the case law, and you cannot resolve the issue in less than an hour, stop and check in with a more senior attorney before devoting more time to the issue.

- **Team Tracker**: Every team member is expected to update the status of their action items in the team tracker every weekday morning by 9 a.m.

- **Retros**: At the end of a matter, the most junior team member is responsible for scheduling time for a retro, taking notes in the meeting, and distributing them to the team.*

- **PTO**: In addition to booking vacation days through our HR system, please note your expected vacations on our team

---

* This team norm is intended to solve the problem of retros not occurring because no one takes the lead on setting them up consistently. Assigning a more junior team member this responsibility tends to result in more reliable execution.

vacation tracker so that we can plan for coverage. This
includes weekends that you anticipate being unavailable.

You might notice some similarities between these examples
and the open-ended questions in Chapter 4 used for developing trust. That is not a coincidence; the more we can encourage
transparency around working styles, the better off everyone is.
Some teams even include team values and other more abstract
expectations in their team norms. Of course, these examples are
just illustrative, but you can see that this kind of documentation
takes the guesswork out of a team's operating rhythm. And for
new team members, it will allow them to find their groove with
the team much faster.

You might think of this as a set of team policies. The only
reason I do not use that phrasing here is that the term "policy"
brings to mind a top-down, bureaucratic pronouncement from
a faceless administrator. Ideally, the team should work *together*
to align on their team norms *with* the team leader, rather than
the team leader dictating these expectations unilaterally. The list
should also be a living document, one that the team revises regularly (such as by reviewing the team norms as part of the retro).
The exercise helps bring the team together and get buy-in around
these commitments.

This is why I liken team norms to a set of social contracts. By
committing to these norms, team members will know what is
expected and find it easier to hold others accountable. After all, it
is much easier to give feedback when expectations are clear.

In fact, clarity is the name of the game across all of the process
improvements we have covered. Below is a summary of these tactics.
Notice how each tactic helps reinforce a culture of accountability.

OPPORTUNITY	TACTICS
Meeting Management	• Set clear agendas (noting expected time for each topic and putting "consult" topics first and "inform" topics last) • Check with the group when going off track (e.g., "tangent alert") to decide whether to allow the deviation or table the issue • Document action items, and ensure each has one name and a deadline attached
Task Tracking	• Use a "tracker" for action items, and make sure the whole team has access • Use a "parking lot" for backburner issues, and revisit quarterly
Retros	• Conduct a thirty- to sixty-minute retrospective after big milestones to capture what worked and what should change for next time • Flag opportunities for future training
Team Norms	• Document expectations for how the team operates, e.g., communication, project management, vacation planning, team values, etc. • Build this document collaboratively and revisit regularly, e.g., during retros

Too often, high-caliber teams with top talent falter in execution because they are not rigorous about project management. This applies to legal cases and deals but also to strategic initiatives within government agencies and private companies.

By running a tight ship, you allow accountability to thrive. Ambiguous expectations, vague deadlines, and chaotic meetings not only make it more difficult to stay on track, but they make it hard to even judge *whether* things are on track or not. I have overseen many teams that could not honestly say if they were meeting expectations because they had been so unclear about their dead-lines and goals from the beginning. If they cannot judge their own progress, imagine how hard it is to be their manager.

These problems are all fixable, but they require the commitment of the entire team, not just the manager. For legal teams, good process is the grease that keeps the engine working smoothly, even at high speed. It also takes the guesswork out of teamwork, reducing the stress that team members feel when trying to figure out how a new team operates. The result: more efficient, happier teams.

Now that team members know how to work together, the next hurdle for accountability is squarely in the hands of managers: autonomy.

CHAPTER 15

AUTONOMY

I n the classic video game Oregon Trail, players donned the role of a wagon leader guiding pioneers from Independence, Missouri, to the Willamette Valley in Oregon while traveling along the Oregon Trail in 1848. The game would require the pioneers to forage for berries, hunt for meat, and, if at all possible, try not to die of snakebite or dysentery along the way.

But one of the most treacherous decisions facing the intrepid wagoneer was how to cross the many rivers on their way to Oregon. Every river was different, and each changed with the season. If shallow enough, one could "ford" the river, meaning the oxen would pull the wagon across with the wheels along the river bottom. If calm enough, one could "caulk" the wagon, essentially converting it to a boat and floating it across. One could even hire a ferry or local guide, depending on the cost. The right decision hinged on the conditions of the river at the time of the crossing, and there was no way to know in advance which choice was the right one.

Imagine managing a team of these Oregon-bound wagoneers, each starting their journey at different times, while you stay behind in Missouri. If you insist on directing every aspect of the trip from afar, you will be in trouble. After all, you cannot predict the best way of crossing each river in advance. If a party has to stop and send someone to ask you for instructions, conditions will change by the time you make a decision. And on top of all that, your micromanagement will rob the wagon leaders of their autonomy. Without that, there is no sense of adventure; there is only "following orders."

Of course, the other extreme is just as dangerous. Without offering some guidance, your teams could end up way off track. They might decide that it would be more lucrative to abandon the trail and pan for gold instead.

Good managers must find a balance. They must provide enough autonomy to let people react to the situation on the ground, and enough guidance to ensure they are equipped to navigate difficult situations and aligned on the ultimate goals.

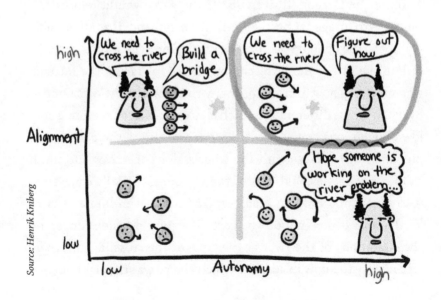

This dilemma exists across every industry, not just law. At Spotify, the global media and technology company, engineering training leader Henrik Kniberg used the illustration on the previous page to explain how their teams approach this dilemma.

When the team has neither autonomy nor alignment—the bottom left box—the workstreams are all fragmented. Think of this like a factory where everyone has a specific job to do, but no one understands how these jobs add up to a whole, and the manager always seems to be on a lunch break when a problem arises. The work quickly becomes directionless and chaotic.

When you have high autonomy but no alignment—the bottom right box—then everyone blissfully does whatever they want. This boundless freedom might make team members happy in the short run, but their disorganized efforts will not help the team reach its goals. Your wagoneers may get distracted on the way to Oregon, avoid the rivers altogether, and open up a general store instead.

At the top left, you have high alignment but low autonomy. This is the realm of micromanagement. The manager explains the problem to solve (we need to cross the river) but also dictates the specific *solution* (build a bridge). The team does not have a chance to come up with their own solutions to the problem, which is how they will learn and grow. Because they never become self-sufficient, the leader is forced to get in the weeds for every new challenge. Too slow; too inefficient.

The top right box is where the magic happens. When you have *high autonomy* and *high alignment*, the team understands the goal but retains some freedom to determine the best way to reach that goal, much like the wagoneer who knows the river must be crossed but can decide the best means based on the conditions on the ground.

This freedom allows the team to be creative, to make decisions more quickly, and to make mistakes—all of which support rapid growth. It is not a free-for-all; the manager must be available to answer questions and review the work so that mistakes can be corrected (i.e., before getting to the client or the court). But the manager no longer *bottlenecks* the team's growth. With this leadership, we can have a nimble, mission-driven team that holds *itself* to high standards, rather than a team that takes all its cues from a manager.

In this chapter, we will dive deeper into the techniques that help managers find this balance. The key is delegation. Delegate too little, and the team does not grow. Too much, and the team becomes overwhelmed. But there are also complications to delegation that are specific to legal work. After all, sometimes the unique timelines and pressures of our profession make delegation risky; no attorney wants to jeopardize a client's goals or their ethical duty of care for the sake of a "learning experience."

This chapter is broken into two parts. First, we will explore the barriers to delegation—that is, what prevents attorneys from delegating in the first place—and how to navigate those roadblocks. But making the decision to delegate is only the first challenge. Next comes the handoff itself, with its own set of pitfalls. Together, these lessons provide a practical guide for managers to create the right level of autonomy on their teams.

BARRIERS TO DELEGATION

You cannot have autonomy without delegation. Delegation provides attorneys the space to own their work and to learn. Mistakes are a part of this learning process, so managers need to allow room for mistakes without putting the final work product at risk.

This risk can be downright frightening. As attorneys, our business not only depends on serving our clients, but we also have an ethical duty of care. It is literally the *first rule* of professional conduct in the ABA's model rules:

> A lawyer shall provide competent representation to a client. Competent representation requires the legal knowledge, skill, thoroughness and preparation reasonably necessary for the representation.[29]

Incompetence is not just bad for business; it's grounds for malpractice. And when an attorney delegates work to another attorney, the supervisor does not "pass off" this responsibility; the supervisor *still* has an ethical duty to ensure the junior attorney's work is competent.[30]

If that weren't enough, attorneys have other reasons for choosing not to delegate, such as:

- "I can do it myself faster than explaining it to someone else."
- "I don't want to burden my already-strapped team."
- "It's 10 p.m. and this is due first thing in the morning."
- "The stakes are too high."
- "The client asked for me specifically."
- "This is too complex for a more junior attorney."

All of these concerns are understandable. But delegation is not a binary yes-or-no decision; delegation is a *process*. When you reframe delegation as a series of steps rather than a single decision, it becomes easier to see how we can navigate these concerns more smoothly.

The process starts with project planning. For intense matters, like fast-paced deals, aggressive litigation timelines, or other sprints, attorneys need to plan ahead so they can avoid situations where delegation becomes impossible due to time constraints. Indeed, time is the most important prerequisite for delegation. Other delegation barriers—like the work being too complex or too "high stakes"—become much easier to manage when attorneys allow time for coaching and iteration. But when time is too limited, delegation becomes impossible.

Before a big push, the managing attorney should sit down with a team and sketch out an expected sequence of events. This timeline should not only include obvious dates (like filing deadlines) but also less obvious milestones that more seasoned attorneys know to expect, such as client check-in meetings, likely negotiation touchpoints with opposing counsel, and windows for partner review. Even if these dates are only "penciled in," they help the team spot bottlenecks ahead of time. For example, these more detailed timelines make clear that a document "due" on the 14th will actually require a first draft on the 9th so that (a) the partner has two days to review, (b) the client has three days after that for final sign-off, and (c) the team has one extra day to incorporate last-minute changes. These details matter.

Our goal is to *reduce the risk* of delegation. More granular timelines do just that because they account for review and iteration time—critical steps for quality control.

Imagine a litigation senior associate wants a junior associate to draft a brief for a motion to compel. It would not be helpful for the senior associate to say, "Today is Monday. We need to get a draft to the client by a week from Friday." That would likely mean the senior associate gets the draft perhaps one day before the deadline—if the senior associate is lucky. Then the senior associate will end up scrambling to make edits (and certainly not have time for coaching the junior associate).

Instead, imagine the senior associate suggests this timeline:

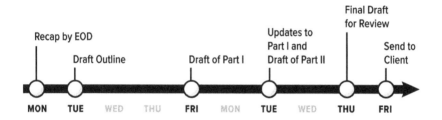

- Today is Monday. Please send me an email by the end of today recapping your understanding of this assignment just to make sure we're on the same page.
- By EOD Tuesday, please send a rough outline of your brief—bullet points only—so that we are aligned on the key issues to address.
- By the end of this week (Friday), please send me a draft of Part I. Don't wait for my response on the outline to begin drafting.
- I will send you comments on Part I by midday Monday. That should give you time to incorporate my edits to Part I and finish a draft of Part II, sending the consolidated draft to me by EOD Tuesday.
- I'll send you comments on your draft by Wednesday evening so that you can turn around a final draft by Thursday. That will give the partner a day to review in case she wants a last look.
- Then we can deliver it to the client Friday.

This conversation yields a much more thoughtful timeline with plenty of check-ins and room for iteration.

That said, the senior associate would be wise not to deliver this timeline as a monologue. Instead, make it a conversation, checking in to confirm that the junior associate thinks the deadlines are reasonable and making adjustments as needed. Or better yet, ask the junior associate to draft the timeline and then offer comments, using it as an opportunity to *teach* project management, rather than dictate it.

Either way, the result is a more granular timeline that breaks up a large assignment into digestible pieces. If there is a problem—for example, if the junior associate misses a major issue in the brief—the senior associate will spot the issue early, likely on Day 2 (upon seeing the outline). Or if the senior associate has not worked with the junior associate before and is unfamiliar with the junior's writing ability, the senior will get a window into that when seeing the draft of Part I on that first Friday. If the writing is unsatisfactory, the senior associate then has an entire week to plan for the additional time that will be needed for coaching and iteration. This is how managing attorneys reduce last-minute scrambling.

Granular timelines are just one way to de-risk delegation. The other is to break up complex tasks into smaller tasks that team members can handle. For example, instead of asking a transactional associate to draft a complex section of an agreement, one might ask the associate first to find several examples of similar clauses and compile a list of key differences. The managing attorney could then review the list with the associate to provide some coaching before asking the associate to create the first draft.

Senior attorneys also fear delegation when they believe the client expects them to attend to the issue personally. For example, suppose a client emails a senior associate asking for perspective on a specific deal term. In that case, the senior associate may feel responsible even though a more junior attorney is just as knowledgeable.

The question is whether the client truly wants the *senior associate's* answer or just *the right answer*, regardless of the source. In my experience, the former is rare (though it does happen). But attorneys should not jump to this conclusion. If attorneys assume that clients always want to hear from them *personally*, then not only do their plates fill up unnecessarily, but more junior associates never get the chance to step up and build client relationships.

If you feel strongly that the client does not want you to delegate, by all means, follow your business instinct. Otherwise, consider a thoughtful pass-off. For example:

Good question, Frank. Let me loop in Melissa, who has been working on the deal term from Day 1 and has extensive experience with issues like this. Melissa, let's touch base on this to make sure Frank gets what he needs.

From then on, Melissa can take the lead, with you CC'ed. The client knows you are still involved, but the matter is largely delegated.

Worried this will rub the client the wrong way? Talk to the client about your concern directly. In fact, use it as an opportunity to check in on the client relationship and communication generally—a trust-building exercise. For example, you might phrase your question to the client this way:

I want to take a step back and check in with you to make sure you are getting what you need from me and the team. Do you feel comfortable with how we have been dividing and conquering? Any concerns about our roles or coordination?

These candid conversations can be powerful client management tools. When I was general counsel at a technology company, neither of the big firms we worked with checked in with me or our CEO regularly to get our feedback. They took us to dinner every few years to talk about current events or ask about our families—a perfectly nice gesture. While that kind of small talk did build friendships (personal trust), it did little to demonstrate that the partners were truly committed to serving us and our goals (professional trust).

Best practices for client management are a subject for another book, but you can see how these kinds of conversations can reduce the risk that delegation will offend the client. Rather than make assumptions about the client's preferences for who does the work, a concerned attorney can simply ask the question directly, building trust and unlocking delegation in one fell swoop.

Despite all of these tactics, there will still be times when delegation remains genuinely impractical. For example, when the truly unexpected happens—such as a last-minute, urgent request from a client—there simply may not be time to delegate the task to someone unfamiliar with how to handle it. The urgent deadline leaves no room for iteration and coaching. In these situations, the manager can and should complete the task personally.

But they should not stop there. Remember, the point of delegation is to create space for *learning*. After the crisis is over, take the time to go back and walk other team members through the issue.

In *Turn the Ship Around!*, David Marquet, a former nuclear submarine commander, described his approach to time-sensitive issues in these words:

- If the decision needs to be made urgently, make it, then have the team [review] the decision and evaluate it.
- If the decision needs to be made reasonably soon, ask for team input, even briefly, then make the decision.
- If the decision can be delayed, then force the team to provide inputs. Do not force the team to come to consensus; that results in whitewashing differences and dissenting votes. Cherish the dissension. If everyone thinks like you, you don't need them.[31]

This is a perfect analogy for how attorneys can approach time-sensitive tasks. In all three scenarios, the leader creates space for the team to learn. Even when the manager must take control of the situation personally—i.e., when delegation is impossible— the team still has a chance to gain something from the experience, albeit after the fact.

In other words, either make time to teach along the way, or make time to teach at the end. If you are a manager who does neither, you will likely wake up one day to find you are both a bottleneck and a micromanager. This is how teams grind to a halt.

For those more junior attorneys on the receiving end of delegated work, you have important lessons to glean here as well. If your manager struggles with delegation, put your ownership mindset to work and consider what *you* can do to make delegation easier. For example, if your manager does not give you granular timelines that take into account checkpoints and iteration, you can draft such timelines yourself. If you know a complex phase of legal work is coming, you can suggest ways to break it down into digestible pieces. And if you want to demonstrate that you can be trusted with complex work, you could send proactive updates like the weekly email described in Chapter 6.* Actions like these will help the managing attorney feel more comfortable giving you additional responsibility.

HANDOFF RISKS

Deciding to delegate is only half the battle. Next comes the actual handoff of work. When a handoff is fumbled, the task usually does not go well. This can have far-reaching implications; for example, the manager may see the act of delegation *itself* as the problem and fall back into old habits of hoarding work, which is a lose-lose for both attorneys. To stay on track, all attorneys should be aware of five common handoff risks—and the tactics for navigating them.

Handoff Risk #1: Delegating Without Context

As a rule of thumb, however much context you think a more junior attorney needs to complete a task successfully—*give more*. Attorneys often hold back context not because they like to be secretive but because they think more junior attorneys simply do not *need* or *want* to know more. But managers can never antici-pate every possible misunderstanding or misstep that might befall the junior attorney. By providing more context, the junior attorney has a better chance of intuiting the right path when the unexpected arises.

For example, a senior associate once asked me to research creative approaches that could allow us to get a favorable docu-ment (hearsay) into evidence. I wrote up a twelve-page memo

---

* See Chapter 6, Scenario #6 ("My manager micromanages me.").

outlining hearsay exceptions and other evidentiary workarounds that might be useful. He said it was an outstanding memo—and completely unnecessary. He had actually already decided the document was unlikely to be admitted and just wanted to ensure he covered his bases before explaining the bad news to the client. He was after client management, not a dissertation.*

When providing context, attorneys usually start with the task at hand and perhaps offer some broader context about the matter itself (i.e., the case, deal, or project). Few go the extra mile to explain how this fits into the client's overall goals, the practice group's strategy, or the firm's vision. But they should.

CONTEXT: THE MORE THE MERRIER

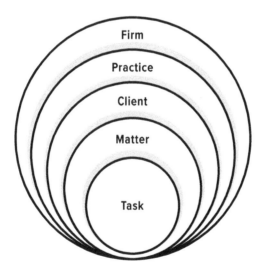

---

* Of course, I could have avoided this outcome myself if I had pushed for parameters earlier. See Chapter 6, Scenario #2 ("My manager does not give clear direction.").

For example, suppose the senior associate who assigned me the evidentiary research question had offered me this additional information:

> The client is pushing us to find a way to get the document into evidence, and we've explained that it's not likely to happen. But to give you a bit more background, the client is not a traditional litigation client. The firm has only done bankruptcy work for them in the past, and our white-collar practice group is trying to expand our relationship. We know they use one of our competitors for most of their litigation and are used to their aggressive style. So this is a bit of a test for us; we need to show them we are just as aggressive. In fact, this is part of the firm's larger strategy to expand our market share within Fortune 100 companies by leveraging our bankruptcy relationships. So far, we've had a lot of success.

In just thirty seconds, the managing attorney's speech not only clarifies the parameters of the task, but it provides a window into the strategy at play behind the scenes.

If you want associates to care about the *firm*—not just the *tasks* assigned to them—bring them into the fold. This peek "behind the curtain" makes attorneys feel less like cogs in a machine and more like equals. For more senior attorneys, this context also gives them a chance to develop their strategic thinking. But even junior associates will appreciate the gesture; it serves as a signal that the managing attorney believes the junior attorney is sophisticated enough to have a place in this conversation.

Managing attorneys should also provide context about how this task connects to other tasks in the project—i.e., dependencies.

For example, is someone else waiting on this work product to incorporate it into their assignment? Who else will be reviewing this task? When attorneys understand the dependencies downstream, they can coordinate with other team members if necessary, especially when they need more time.

Handoff Risk #2: Delegating Without Guardrails

In Chapter 8, we talked about how great leaders cultivate an ownership mentality on their teams by delegating tasks—a preview for the broader themes we are discussing in this chapter. We also noted that delegation requires *guardrails*. Now we will sharpen this guidance even further with specific types of guardrails that attorneys should consider when handing off tasks: time-boxing, scope constraints, resource support, and relief valves.

The first two—time-boxing and scope constraints—are about *focus*. "Time-boxing" a task means providing specific guidance around how much time you believe the task ought to take. Of course, you may not know how long an assignment should take, so attorneys will typically use time-boxing as a check-in tool. (E.g., "If you spend more than two hours on this, stop and check in with me.")

By contrast, "scope constraints" create focus around the subject matter. This could include the obvious, such as clarifying the jurisdiction, or the less obvious, such as noting that, if the attorney wanders into obscure environmental regulations, those issues should be left alone because another team has them covered. Scope constraints could also include informing the attorney about decisions that have already been made—such as particular arguments in or out of scope—that might be relevant to the task. As suggested earlier, the more context, the better.

The next two tactics are helpful in situations where attorneys have trouble getting the project done within the guardrails—that is, within the time or scope constraints.

For starters, the managing attorney can offer guidance on "resource support." The managing attorney might note that, if needed, the junior attorney can leverage specific paralegals or other attorneys who have experience in this area and may have time to help. Resource support is particularly important for technical issues, such as when attorneys are asked to ramp up on specialized e-discovery software, analyze a complex data set, or become fluent in the subject of a patent. The managing attorney can give specific suggestions on precisely *who* can offer expertise on *which* subjects. This can include internal IT contacts, other colleagues, client-side experts, and even third-party vendors. If attorneys have to "ask around" to find these resources when the need arises, they will waste valuable time.

Next, for tasks where the manager knows the assignment might be difficult to complete in the time allotted, the managing attorney can proactively talk the junior attorney through potential "relief valves." For example, suppose a client asked for a briefing on a new piece of legislation, but the team is already crunched for time on another matter for the same client. The managing attorney might hand off the request to an associate with this caveat:

> I'd like you to spend no more than six hours on this. I know that will be tricky, so let's proceed this way. Ideally, we would put together a presentation for the client and walk them through it formally. Let's have that goal in mind, but first, start with just compiling a one-page set of talking points in an outline format. If you get that done within two to three hours,

use the remaining time to turn that into polished slides. If not, just do your best to convert your one-page outline into a handout, and we'll make that work for a more informal discussion.

In this example, the presentation is the primary task; the bullet-point handout is the contingency plan. This provides a relief valve if time is running low.

Common relief valves attorneys might consider include:

- Reducing the scope of the request (e.g., focusing on issue X and coming back to Y and Z later)
- Reducing the level of formality (e.g., bullet points rather than a formal memo)
- Requesting more time (e.g., whether it might be possible to ask the client, court, or other parties for more time, and the trade-offs in doing so)

Managers, do not wait until a problem arises to offer relief valves. It is best to talk through these options in advance—at the handoff stage itself—thereby giving the attorney as complete a toolkit as possible for success. Some managing attorneys may be concerned that talking through potential relief valves in advance (such as the possibility of reducing scope or formality) will encourage the attorney to fall back to those easier "Plan B" options without even trying for "Plan A." Perhaps, but instead of eliminating these tools—effectively asking the attorney to work with one hand tied behind the back—consider entrusting the attorney to make the right decision. Then, later, if you feel the attorney pulled the lever on those relief valves too early, start a dialogue about that decision. Embrace the opportunity for coaching.

Relief valves are a great teaching tool; they demonstrate advanced project management skills in action. After all, attorneys routinely have to adjust the scope of their legal work when they lack the time to research every issue perfectly. Deciding how best to make these trade-offs, given the client's goals and our ethical duty of competence, requires careful judgment. One of my favorite executives once quipped that for any question you might ask him in his subject area, no matter how complex, he could always give you a two-week answer, a two-day answer, or a *two-hour* answer. (I'm pretty sure he could give a solid two-minute answer too.) He meant that he could calibrate his level of precision and depth based solely on time constraints, a kind of mental flexibility that is rare (and sought-after, especially in the business world). I have worked with attorneys who were unable to make these trade-offs; every task that *could* take two weeks *did* take two weeks, and the only way to speed things up was to skip food and sleep—an unsustainable solution.

These four mechanisms—time-boxing, scope constraints, resource support, and relief valves—help attorneys manage complex assignments within a set of guardrails. In addition, attorneys might also consider a "surface, don't solve" rule as a kind of "catch-all" guardrail. This guidance—first introduced in the section on ownership*—helps reduce rabbit holes by asking associates to let the *managing attorney* decide whether unexpected issues should be addressed or ignored. But there is a drawback: this rule sets up the managing attorney as a gatekeeper. As much as possible, managers should strive to provide enough guidance for junior attorneys to handle most challenges

---

* See Chapter 7, Scenario #4 ("They get stuck on things that don't matter.").

on their own. Keep this in mind when deciding what guardrails to use when making your handoff.

Handoff Risk #3: Delegating Without Prioritizing

Attorneys rarely work on just one matter at a time. Even within a specific matter, attorneys usually own more than one task. So when a manager hands off a new task to an attorney, that attorney has to make a call about how best to prioritize the new task against everything else on the attorney's plate.

This is not a simple exercise; deciding how to balance tasks within and across matters is like comparing apples and oranges in the middle of a pie-eating contest. Calling this an exercise in "time management" oversimplifies the challenge and overlooks an important teaching opportunity.

Instead, when handing off a new task, managing attorneys should ask the person about other priorities. This starts with asking about other tasks on this matter but does not end there. The manager should also inquire about other matters the attorney is working on and discuss the implications of adding more to the person's plate.

If the manager is a senior associate, chances are the person is not in a position to decide how to balance commitments on this matter with commitments on entirely different matters under another partner. But even in these situations, senior associates can be incredibly helpful. First, they can simply be thought partners, talking through the different obligations and helping the more junior attorney come up with a plan of attack. Second, in times when junior associates seem genuinely overwhelmed, senior associates may be able to leverage their network within the firm, talk to the right partners, and help find a solution. One of my mentors was famous for calling two partners on a three-way call and prompting them to discuss which of their matters would take priority—a life-saving feat that most junior associates would find far too intimidating to do on their own.

In addition to discussing other matters, the managing attorney should ask about any personal time commitments or PTO that might come into play during the course of the assignment. I will never forget the partner who walked into my office on a Friday at 5 p.m. and handed me a task, saying, "Not to worry—you have all weekend to work on this." Even though I have spent my entire career in jobs that routinely required working late nights and long weekends, the unapologetic implication that my weekend *belonged* to the firm sent a cold message. By contrast, asking about PTO and personal commitments shows that a manager cares about work-life balance.

I want to pause here to emphasize that junior attorneys do not always get to put their PTO and personal commitments first. There will be times when attorneys must make sacrifices; that is a fact of life in our industry. So when I say that managers should ask about PTO and personal commitments, that does not entitle junior attorneys to a "get out of work free" card. The point is to generate a *dialogue*. If at all possible, the manager should try to respect those commitments. And in the rare cases where this is not possible, the manager should explain the situation and be appreciative—not presumptuous.

Finally, as part of the prioritization conversation, managing attorneys should also ask about the attorney's personal priorities and goals—especially development goals. For example, if the attorney's last review suggested the need to practice a particular skill, that would be good information for the managing attorney to know. If possible, the managing attorney can assign tasks based on those priorities, or at least shape the task to create the best possible learning opportunity.

Prioritization conversations are an incredibly important—and routinely overlooked—part of the delegation process. They help avoid bottlenecks, build trust, and perhaps most importantly, reduce *burnout*.

Attorneys are especially prone to burnout because they often work for several different managers at once, none of whom see the complete picture of their fragmented workload. Stress can build invisibly in this situation until the attorney's only escape is to quit. Managers can use the delegation handoff as an opportunity to open a dialogue about these issues. Then, if appropriate, they can surface concerns to partners, HR, and others who can help.

Avoiding burnout is particularly important for underrepresented attorneys because they often lack the networks others have in the organization. Without those resources, their stress may go unnoticed and unaddressed for longer, yet another contributor to attrition. Managers should be sensitive to these implications and be proactive about helping attorneys navigate these challenges. Otherwise, without a thoughtful, open conversation about priorities, many overwhelmed attorneys will conceal their stress to preserve an image of resilience.

Handoff Risk #4: Delegating to the Same People

Everyone has "favorites" at work—people who are a delight to work with and have been reliable time and time again. When a managing attorney has to decide who will take on a particular task, many will default to their favorites first. This is entirely understandable—but also dangerous.

Delegating to the same people over and over creates two distinct problems. First, it places the greatest burden on your highest performers, which means that your best team members are the *most* likely to burn out first. No one wants that. Second, even when this favoritism is ostensibly based on prior performance, unconscious bias can still worm its way into a manager's judgment. As we noted in earlier chapters, managers tend to favor people who look, think, communicate, and behave the same way they would.

Bias in assignments tends to manifest most often when a manager makes such decisions "on the fly." Instead, a managing attorney should keep careful track of which tasks are assigned to which team members, and then check this list before assigning new tasks to ensure balance. If managers maintain a robust tracker—as suggested in the previous chapter—this is an easy exercise.

Of course, managers cannot simply hand out work like a poker dealer passing out one card at a time around a circle. Sometimes the best person for the job is the person already working on a related task, and achieving a perfect balance of work is extremely difficult. But the process does not require mathematical precision. The managing attorney need only be *mindful* of the overall balance of assignments when making decisions. That one extra step can lead to a much more equitable spread of work across the team.

I know it would be foolish to suggest that attorneys stop having favorite people at the office; that would be like asking someone to stop being human. Instead, I ask managers simply to be *aware* of their biases. Leaders have a responsibility to teach and support *everyone*. That does not mean everyone will succeed, but everyone deserves access to the kind of teaching and support that puts them in a position to be successful.

Handoff Risk #5: Not Accounting for Working Style Differences

In Chapter 3, we explored how differences in working styles, confidence, background, and more can affect our approach to work. By acknowledging these differences, we can overcome common impediments to trust and support stronger, more diverse teams.

These differences are particularly important when delegating work. During the handoff conversation, imagine a manager who thoughtfully explains the task—its nuances, timelines, and implications. Then the manager ends this monologue by asking, "Do you have any questions?"

What happens next might vary from attorney to attorney. Those who can process information instantly and have the confidence to ask questions on the spot may have no trouble engaging in an immediate dialogue to sharpen their understanding of the assignment. But some attorneys lack the confidence to raise questions right then and there, for fear of looking incompetent. Others may need time to digest the information before even knowing *whether* they have questions. And when questions do arise later, some attorneys have a strong peer network they can leverage for help without having to "bother the boss," while others do not. As we have discussed, attorneys from underrepresented groups are more likely to face many of these barriers.

Managing attorneys should never assume that silence equals understanding. There are several tips for avoiding this trap:

- After explaining assignments to more junior attorneys, ask them to recap their understanding via email after the meeting
- Ask how they plan to approach the task, giving you a chance to hear their thought process (and spot issues)

- Check in the next day after they have had time to get started; ask about their progress and any additional questions they have
- Do not ask: "Do you have any questions?" Instead, try: "What questions do you have?"

These small tweaks can have a tremendous impact. By accounting for differences in working styles, managing attorneys can ensure a smoother handoff of work across the board. Ignoring these issues, on the other hand, can exacerbate systemic barriers.

It may seem that we have ventured a long way from the Oregon Trail, so let's take a moment to review how we got here. To create a culture of *accountability*, we need team members to feel a sense of *autonomy*. To create space for autonomy, attorneys have to embrace *delegation*. And to delegate effectively, attorneys have to ensure a smooth *handoff* of work.

So much of an attorney's skill in delegation relies on a good handoff. Below is a summary of the tactics just discussed:

HANDOFF RISKS	SOLUTIONS
Delegating without context	• Consider not just the task and matter but the client, practice group, and firm strategy
Delegating without guardrails	• Time estimates/time-boxing (e.g., "If you spend more than two hours, check in with me.") • Scope constraints (e.g., issues to avoid, decisions that were already made) • Resource support (e.g., if needed, leverage paralegals, other associates, vendors) • Relief valves (e.g., reducing scope, reducing formality, requesting more time) • Also helpful: a "surface, don't solve" rule

HANDOFF RISKS	SOLUTIONS
Delegating without prioritizing	• Discuss other priorities within the project • Discuss the person's priorities outside the project • Talk about expected personal time or PTO constraints • Ask about other personal priorities and goals
Delegating to the same people	• Ensure balance across the team by tracking and reviewing assignments before delegating new tasks • Be aware of your own biases and "favorites," and remember that a manager's job is to teach
Not accounting for working style differences	• Ask the attorney to recap the assignment via email after the meeting • Ask how the attorney plans to approach the task, giving you a chance to hear the thought process (and spot issues) • Check in the next day after work has begun, asking about progress and offering to answer any additional questions • Avoid: "Do you have any questions?" Instead, try: "What questions do you have?"

If organizations or practice groups want to up their delegation game even further, they can adopt a teamwide template for delegation conversations.* A consistent approach to delegation across managers helps avoid mistakes, cuts out idiosyncrasies, and reduces bias.

ALL ROADS LEAD BACK TO TRUST

When you nail delegation, you provide attorneys the autonomy they need to thrive in their work. But all of this depends on trust. If managers cannot trust their teams, delegation breaks down, and autonomy dissolves along with it.

---

* A sample template is available online at *allrisebook.com*.

For those on remote or hybrid legal teams, this lesson is especially important. Remote work can have benefits under the right conditions. But research during the COVID-19 pandemic showed that when autonomy is low and micromanagement is high because of *managerial mistrust*, those benefits are unlikely to materialize.[32] Again and again, we see that all roads lead back to trust.

This undercurrent of trust will be even more important in the next chapter as we complete our trifecta for accountability: we covered project management and autonomy; next, we dive into *feedback*.

CHAPTER 16

CREATING A CULTURE OF CONTINUOUS FEEDBACK

Many years ago, I was frustrated with a fellow vice president for holding back the team's growth. At the time, we were both VPs in two different departments, and I had to deal with his dominating behavior in meetings again and again. Everyone talked about it—his direct reports, his colleagues, and I would complain to each other about how he would get so excited about his own ideas that he would interrupt other people and take over the conversation. Collaborating with him seemed unbearable.

Finally, I decided to sit him down in a room and lay out all of my grievances. I chose a small conference room just big enough for two people and a fern. It was called the Zen Room, an ironic title given my intentions. When the meeting started, I let him have it. I recounted a year's worth of examples of his behavior and pointed out how his lack of EQ was driving the team crazy. In response, he barely said a word. In that room, he became just another potted plant.

The next day, he pulled me aside to talk again. He said that he stayed up all night thinking about what I had said. He never realized others saw him that way, and he felt terrible. His eyes were glassy as he spoke. He promised he would change. And true to his word, over the next twelve months, he went from being my mortal enemy to a world-class executive and one of my most trusted colleagues for the next several years.

Looking back, he wasn't the real problem. I was.

For more than a year, his behavior had ruffled feathers, and for more than a year, his colleagues—and I, an executive who should know better—simply complained about him behind his back. No one gave him feedback because we all assumed it would be pointless. And when I finally did talk to him, I attacked. There was nothing mature about my approach, nothing reflecting the principles of this book. If there was any maturity in the room that day in the Zen Room, it was his.

When we bottle up our feedback, we rob others of a chance to grow. As attorneys, we need feedback. We crave it. And not just about our legal work but about our management style, our communication, project planning, and more. But often this feedback does not materialize. Or when it does, the delivery may be so poor that we have to sift through the garbage to find the gold nuggets—as my colleague had to do when I unleashed my unproductive diatribe. (It was a miracle he was able to turn my mistake into something positive—a testament to his greater capacity for introspection at the time.)

This incident with my fellow VP was the wake-up call I needed to reshape my relationship with feedback. Over the subsequent years, I began to think about feedback with an entirely different mindset, which I then shared with my teams. I realized that feedback is not a privilege; it is a right. Our colleagues have the right to hear and learn from our feedback, and we have an obligation to provide it. It is an implicit part of the job description—every job description. This obligation does not begin or end with managers; it is universal. This is because feedback should flow in all directions, including upward feedback, downward feedback, and peer feedback.

The strongest teams live by these principles every day, and their growth has no ceiling. But it is a tall order. There are many barriers to building such a culture, especially on legal teams. But it can be done.

This chapter will explain how to build this feedback culture brick by brick. First, there will be a few prerequisites that every team needs to understand before committing to this transformation. Next, leaders need to paint a picture of what they want to achieve—a *continuous feedback culture*—and explain precisely what that means. At that point, the attention can turn to specific tactics, with frameworks for difficult conversations and examples of common mistakes lawyers make in giving feedback. Finally, this chapter will close with tips for encouraging a freer flow of feedback, including upward, downward, and peer feedback.

PREREQUISITES FOR THE TRANSFORMATION

Building a strong feedback culture does not happen overnight; it is a process of transformation.

I do not use the word "transformation" for dramatic effect; I do so to set expectations. Even if teams learn the best practices for sharing feedback, they are unlikely to use these skills unless they have already developed the traits we covered in the prior chapters of this book.

To demonstrate how much distance there is to travel, I often ask attorneys whether they freely give candid, constructive feedback to their *superiors*. This is my favorite test for a strong feedback culture. Before they answer, I clarify precisely what I mean: I am not talking about anonymous upward feedback delivered through an HR-approved 360 feedback program once a year; I am asking about truly organic, face-to-face feedback.

For example, if I am talking to a midlevel associate, I will ask if the associate can think of a time when a senior associate or partner said something in a team meeting that rubbed the team the wrong way. (That garners an easy "yes.") Then I will ask if the associate knocked on the more senior attorney's door later and shared that observation as feedback. The response to that is usually some version of silent bewilderment. (One associate told me, "That's the craziest thing I've ever heard.")

That kind of behavior is virtually *nonexistent* in law firms. But it is the *norm* in many other industries.

Wherever you are today, you will probably not be able to go from "here" to "there" in a single bound. That is because many other high-performance traits contribute to a strong feedback culture. We need those foundations in place before reaching for the sky.

Consider how a lack of trust, ownership, and conflict can stand in the way of a free exchange of feedback:

- Without *trust*, team members do not share feedback either because they fear looking like "jerks" or because they think others' mistakes are examples of immutable character flaws—the fundamental attribution error—making feedback pointless.
- Without a broader sense of *ownership*, team members stay in their lanes, only giving feedback when required to do so by HR. The idea of giving unsolicited feedback—especially upward feedback or peer feedback—outside of the formal HR process carries too much professional risk.
- If teams do not embrace *conflict*, they sugarcoat their feedback. Or, at the other extreme, bottled-up feedback boils over into destructive conflicts because team members lack the skills for navigating difficult conversations.

All of the investment teams make in these other high-performance traits will make it easier to unlock feedback.

The next prerequisite to consider is a common set of expectations. Think of this like a feedback-specific version of the team norms we discuss in Chapter 14. If we do not align on expectations for what "good" feedback looks like, we cannot hold team members accountable on this journey.

As a starting point, consider these four expectations that reflect the best feedback cultures.

Expectation #1: Quality Feedback Must Be Concrete, Actionable, and Supportive

Teams have to align on a definition of "quality" feedback. First, quality feedback is *concrete*, meaning it contains specific examples of behavior. There is nothing more frustrating in a feedback conversation than hearing someone share a generalization and sputter when asked to give specific examples. People need specifics; that is what enables reflection.

Second, quality feedback is *actionable*. This means the feedback should focus on something the person can improve. For example, "tighten up your writing" is too vague to be useful. Similarly, "you are careless" attacks a person's character; that wording suggests the person lacks the *capability* to be careful. People cannot change who they are. Instead, focus on *behavior* and offer specific guidance.

Finally, quality feedback is *supportive*—meaning it is given with the intention to help. The assumption of good intentions, which first appeared in Chapter 2, cuts two ways in feedback conversations. On the one hand, any attorney who gives a colleague feedback should use the assumption of good intentions to avoid mistakes like the fundamental attribution error. This helps ensure feedback is delivered constructively, not destructively. But on the other hand, the *receiver* of the feedback also needs to assume good intentions on the part of the *giver* of feedback. The most common reason attorneys withhold feedback is fear of "looking like a jerk." That is psychological safety (or lack thereof) in action. So if you want candid feedback—and I have never met an attorney who did not—then you as the potential feedback recipient must be ready to embrace the feedback. If someone overcomes their fear and delivers feedback—and it is received well—they will be more likely to do so again in the future.

We will return to these three prongs of quality feedback—*concrete*, *actionable*, and *supportive*—again when we talk about the COIN framework for delivering feedback.

Expectation #2: Growth Requires Both
Positive and Constructive Feedback

When we think of "feedback," we usually imagine constructive feedback. In fact, whenever I would deliver formal reviews, my team members generally hand-waved over the positive feedback and wanted to get straight to constructive areas—"the good stuff," as they called it.

But positive feedback is just as essential as—if not more important than—constructive feedback. People reach their highest level of success by building on their strengths, not by eliminating their weaknesses. Positive feedback also ensures that team members do not waste time trying to fix what is not broken, and it allows them to develop self-confidence along the way.

Remember this maxim from Chapter 8: well-managed teams focus on accomplishing goals; micromanaged teams focus on *avoiding errors*. Exclusively focusing on what someone is doing wrong just feeds into this pathology.

But this does not mean that you have to pair constructive feedback with something positive, or worse yet, "sandwich" positive feedback around constructive feedback. This makes the positive feedback seem like it is only there to cushion the blow. The recipient will then ignore the positive feedback (and likely judge the manager as disingenuous and conflict-avoidant).

Positive feedback can also come off disingenuous when it is vague, so be as concrete as possible, just as with constructive feedback. For example, telling a litigator that you "appreciate all the hard work the last few weeks" can seem patronizing, even if intended genuinely. On the other hand, imagine how a litigator would appreciate hearing more specific praise, e.g., "I was reading your section of the brief, and the way you used the *Johnson* case to tear apart their argument on damages was so clean, I wish I'd thought of it."

People often ask me about the appropriate medium for positive feedback. Unlike constructive feedback, which is best shared live (either in person or virtually) to encourage a dialogue, positive feedback can be just as—if not more—effective when done in writing, such as in an email or via chat. When we share positive feedback in person, many recipients will feel compelled to wave it off or make a self-deprecating joke. But when reading positive feedback alone, they take the time to appreciate the moment. I know many colleagues that save their most adulatory emails in a special folder for posterity.

One final note specifically for junior attorneys: remember that managers need positive feedback too. This is not about stroking egos or brown-nosing. I have seen partners spend years trying to improve their management style, and when associates never take the time to acknowledge the progress, it can feel like that hard work has been in vain. That can cause them to fall back into their old ways. If you like what you are seeing, say something. Reinforce the direction and help the manager build momentum.

Expectation #3: Feedback Should Flow in All Directions, Regardless of Seniority

Feedback is not supposed to flow in just one direction—from the supervisor down to the subordinate. Instead, feedback should flow in both directions, upward and downward. It should also flow between peers, such as attorneys on the same team or partners across practice groups. Your peers are more likely than anyone to understand what you are going through, and they can serve as a fount of information and perspective.

When I teach this principle—especially the part about upward feedback—some attorneys point out that they are there to learn *from* partners, not the other way around. How can they be expected to have suggestions for partners on how to litigate cases better or run better deals?

The answer is to avoid thinking about feedback as being limited to "the legal stuff." Senior attorneys need—and rarely get—feedback about their *management* style. Think about all of the principles we have discussed in this book; you would be hard-pressed to find anyone who nails them all every day. Managers need feedback to improve just like anyone else.

That said, the idea of providing candid feedback to more senior attorneys can be daunting. People may worry that giving such feedback could have repercussions for their relationships or their careers, for example. Managers must not dismiss these fears. When attorneys have not experienced a healthy, free-flowing feedback culture, one cannot simply expect them to leap into the deep end. Moreover, many attorneys have had a history of *negative* experiences watching superiors refuse to admit mistakes and otherwise become defensive in feedback conversations. And underrepresented attorneys, especially women and people of color, may have experienced backlash in the past when trying to bring constructive feedback to a superior's attention.

We have discussed concerns like these already, such as in Chapter 8 in our discussion of backlash. Managers, if you want to encourage the free flow of upward feedback, you cannot just demand it; you have to take the time to understand these fears and build trust. If you are unsure how to proceed, ask a colleague or reach out to your HR or professional development team.

Expectation #4: Formal Reviews Should Not Contain Surprises

Of all the expectations I set with my teams, this last one is the most effective at creating accountability because it is so concrete. In a strong feedback culture, colleagues share feedback throughout the year, such that the formal review should not contain any surprises. That is, if you are writing a piece of feedback in a formal review that you never took the time to share with the attorney before that moment, a red flag should go up in your mind.

This is because we should be building a *continuous feedback culture*. This type of culture ideally includes three stages of feedback. First, there is real-time feedback, which should occur in the natural course of collaboration. Additionally, attorneys meet one-on-one in dedicated feedback sessions for richer, two-way exchanges of feedback. And finally, there is the formal, HR-approved review that typically happens once or twice a year; that review synthesizes all the feedback from the recent period and scores the person's performance against expectations.

Of these three stages of feedback, attorneys tend to be the least familiar with the concept of dedicated feedback sessions. This is a practice I picked up at BCG that became a staple of my management style thereafter: with each of my direct reports—and even with select peers, such as fellow executives with whom I wanted a strong feedback relationship—I set up a recurring meeting every four to six weeks for the purpose of exchanging feedback.* Feedback sessions are for two-way *feedback*; avoid the temptation to lapse into a discussion of the latest tactical issues. Sometimes,

---

* For new team members, I might meet every two weeks for the first two months, then taper back. For veterans with whom I had extremely strong relationships, I might extend to every eight weeks.

you might not have extensive feedback to exchange. But by dedicating the time to feedback, you can ensure open lines of communication and nip issues in the bud early, before they fester.

CONTINUOUS FEEDBACK CULTURE

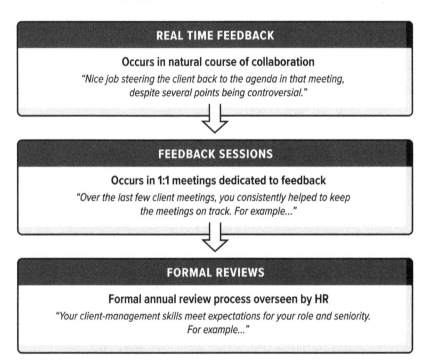

REAL TIME FEEDBACK

Occurs in natural course of collaboration

"Nice job steering the client back to the agenda in that meeting, despite several points being controversial."

FEEDBACK SESSIONS

Occurs in 1:1 meetings dedicated to feedback

"Over the last few client meetings, you consistently helped to keep the meetings on track. For example..."

FORMAL REVIEWS

Formal annual review process overseen by HR

"Your client-management skills meet expectations for your role and seniority. For example..."

I recognize that people need to walk before they run, so if you are still trying to conquer the basics of feedback, recurring feedback sessions might seem overwhelming. But over time, consider implementing this best practice with your team members.

Without feedback sessions, attorneys who are too busy to exchange real-time feedback have no other outlet to share their comments until formal review season, which leads to those dreaded "surprises" in formal reviews. By the time the formal review is delivered, it could be months—sometimes more than a year—after the events you wrote about actually took place. If you want to improve in a particular area, the best way to do so is to receive real-time feedback over the course of several months about that issue. Can you imagine Serena Williams becoming #1 in the world if she only met with her tennis coach once a year to review all her matches?

All my zealousness aside, the "no surprises" rule is a bit aspirational. There will be times when you sit down to write a review and kick yourself as you realize you never said to the person's face what you are about to put in writing. The point of the rule is to remind you to do better next time. In a team that strives to implement the "no surprises" rule, the feedback culture is exceptional.

SUMMARY: COMMON TENETS OF
A STRONG FEEDBACK CULTURE

1. Quality feedback is concrete, actionable, and supportive.
2. Growth requires both positive and constructive feedback.
3. Feedback should flow in all directions, regardless of seniority.
4. Formal reviews should not contain surprises.

Teams need to adopt a common set of expectations about feedback, or they will never achieve the feedback culture they want. Managers, consider sitting down with your teams to align on feedback expectations, using the tenets I laid out as a starting point. This dialogue can also serve as an opportunity to highlight barriers to feedback, especially trust barriers—a perfect team-building session.

BETTER FEEDBACK THROUGH COIN

When we give feedback, the teaching mindset discussed in Chapter 7 is crucial, such as engaging in a dialogue, asking thoughtful questions, looking for specific examples, and more. With this mentality in place, we can simplify the task of delivering constructive feedback using a more structured framework known as COIN: Context, Observations, Impact, and Next Steps.

Context

First, set the stage for feedback. Attorneys sometimes treat feedback as something they can just slip into another conversation. If you try to squeeze in a note of feedback as someone is getting out of a taxi, you will not land your point. Make sure it is the right time and place for feedback and that you have the person's full attention. The weightier the feedback, the more important it is to create that space. The key is to make sure the person is ready and able to engage in what you have to say without distractions.

Observations

As you explain your feedback, start with just the facts, removing emotion and interpretation. Focus on specific actions, not generalizations. For example, do not say that the attorney "lacks attention to detail" or "seems disorganized." These statements judge the person, rather than their actions. Note how this emphasis on specific actions perfectly aligns with the first prong in our earlier definition of quality feedback: being *concrete*. For example, imagine a litigation associate who spent too much time in a rabbit hole on unnecessary issues. Instead of saying the attorney has "trouble prioritizing"—a leap to judgment—start with a more direct observation: "On the motion to dismiss, you addressed core issues A and B, but you also spent time on issues X and Y, which you may not have realized were out of scope because of [this reason]."

Impact

Now comes the "so what." Here, you explain how the behavior you just described affected the team or the outcome. Again, it is important to be specific. For example, let's continue with the scenario above. The manager might describe the impact this way: "Because of the additional time you spent on those out-of-scope issues, Jack and I had to stay up late incorporating your research, and we did not get as much time to edit as we would have liked."

Note that conclusory impact statements like "this won't fly with the client" or "our clients expect better" are not instructive. What do you mean it "won't fly"—why not? When you say clients expect better, what do they expect, specifically? If you do not clarify, you create more questions than answers.

Next Steps

Up until this point, we have been talking only about what happened in the past. Now we shift toward the future. The "N" in COIN stands for "next steps," meaning guidance for how to handle these kinds of situations going forward. This part of the conversation is intended to be a dialogue, not a monologue. Rather than leaping to your own suggestions, you might start with open-ended questions, such as asking about the other person's original intentions—especially if you are giving feedback about interpersonal behavior. This is also the time for you—as the person *giving* the feedback—to ask for ideas on how you can be helpful in the future.

This guidance should be as constructive as possible. For example, continuing our earlier scenario, the manager might say, "Next time, try letting me know if you run into any unexpected issues so that I can weigh in on whether those issues are important or out of scope." But in addition to this advice, the manager might also ask, "Could I have done a better job of clarifying the scope up front? How could I help you avoid these kinds of rabbit holes in the future?"

Let's put all this together. Below is a summary of COIN along with a new scenario on the right-hand side—this time, an example of upward feedback for a perfunctory leader of a deal team.

CONTEXT	Set the stage for this conversation.	*"I want to share some feedback from our recent deal team meeting."*
OBSERVATIONS	Focus on the facts, removing emotion and interpretation.	*"When I shared my concerns about the pace of diligence, you waved your hand and moved on to the next topic. I did not get a chance to explain what I meant."*
IMPACT	Explain the "so what," e.g., how the behavior affected others.	*"That gesture felt dismissive. I took it as a sign I should not share concerns like this in the future."*
NEXT STEPS	Turn this into a *discussion* about what could be different next time. • "Next time, try..." • "Does what I said make sense?" • "What was your intention?" • "How can I help?"	*"Next time, if someone brings up a concern, you could embrace the conversation to show that no topics are off limits."* *"Does that make sense? Would it have been better if I gave you a heads-up beforehand?"*

You can see how COIN supports our tenets of great feedback. It is *concrete* because we are focused on examples and observations. It is *actionable* because we are focused on behavior that the person can change, not jumping to general conclusions about their character or ability to perform. And it is supportive because we are approaching this person with the intention to teach and to help—as a dialogue, not a diatribe.

Now that we have outlined this framework, consider three examples of problematic feedback below and their COIN-friendly counterparts on the right.

POOR FEEDBACK	CONSTRUCTIVE FEEDBACK
"You seem disorganized." ➡	"I found it difficult to follow the flow of your brief. Can you talk me through your outlining process?"
"You are too timid in meetings." ➡	"When the client asked about your section, you deferred to me to answer. I'm curious why. That seemed like a great opportunity to build your credibility. "
"You aren't being collaborative." ➡	"When you rejected Mike's idea without explanation, did you notice how he visibly stiffened? It happened in meeting X and Y as well. Next time..."

In each of the "problematic" examples—all of which are based on real employee reviews—the language is too general and seems to judge the person, rather than actions. The person has the quality of being too "disorganized," "timid," or "uncollaborative." This language is neither concrete nor actionable. By contrast, the improved language on the right addresses these limitations by getting more specific—and inviting dialogue.

Also, feedback on interpersonal behavior can be triggering. Women and people of color are more likely to receive negative feedback when they deviate from social norms—e.g., being perceived as "too aggressive" or "not smiling enough." They are also more likely to hear such feedback as "speak up more in meetings" without taking into account the barriers and backlash to doing so. We talked through many of those considerations in Chapter 8. With COIN (and a bit of awareness), attorneys can engage in more thoughtful, more actionable feedback conversations.

ENCOURAGING CANDID FEEDBACK

Having a framework like COIN can better equip attorneys for delivering feedback. But there is still one last barrier to overcome: *trust*. Just because people know how to give feedback does not mean they will always take advantage of the opportunity.

I saw this firsthand when asking my direct reports for upward feedback. All of the frameworks in the world were not going to make my team members instantly trust me; I would need to earn that trust over time. But the same is true for downward feedback. Many of the attorneys I coach admit that they are often afraid to give candid feedback because they do not want to damage relationships with attorneys, especially when they are working on teams where burnout is a concern. They worry that candid feedback will make morale *worse*.

If you are in a situation where you are not receiving the kind of quality feedback you need to grow—whether that be downward feedback, peer feedback, or upward feedback—there are steps you can take to bring the other person to the table.

I think of this process as a gradual escalation. First—and perhaps most importantly—you have to give the person plenty of warning that you will ask for feedback. Set up time in advance and be clear that you would like to use the time to hear the other person's feedback. If you ask for feedback out of nowhere, you are not likely to get the most thoughtful answer. (Remember the first prong of COIN—Context? As a feedback recipient, you too can help set the stage.)

Second, you can communicate a feedback agenda. For example, you might tell them that you want to get their feedback on specific topics, such as how well you structure your writing, your client management skills, or other specific development areas. As an executive, I even used to ask for feedback on *how well I give feedback*.

If that still does not work, you can move to the third tactic: seeding the conversation. This is a way of softening the ground a bit by acknowledging your own development areas, essentially calling out the elephant in the room. For example, once a year, after I received my formal review, I would meet with each member of my team and read my key areas for development out loud. I'd explain that I agree with every bit of feedback, and then I would ask if they would help me improve by sharing any examples they had observed in the past and continue to share examples in the future. Over the next few months, my direct reports tended to be more comfortable sharing feedback related to those development areas.

Finally, if all else fails, you can "give feedback on feedback." That is, you can explain that you want the person's candid feedback, but so far, you have not been successful. Then open a dialogue, including asking if there is anything you could do to make them more comfortable sharing feedback.

Most of the time, steady escalation through these steps will open the floodgates. Once you finally start receiving genuine feedback, capitalize on that momentum. Follow up regularly and ask if you are making progress in those areas. This is one of the reasons I suggest regular one-on-one "feedback sessions" dedicated to feedback every four to six weeks—to keep the trail of feedback from going cold.

TIPS FOR SOLICITING BETTER FEEDBACK

GIVE PLENTY OF WARNING	"Next Tuesday, I put thirty minutes on your calendar to discuss feedback. I can move it back if you need more time to prepare."
SET A FEEDBACK AGENDA	"Next feedback session, I'd be interested in specific feedback on X, Y, and Z, on top of anything else you want to discuss."
SEED THE CONVERSATION	"I'd like your thoughts on how I handled the last few client calls. Sometimes, I worry I am pushing too hard. What do you think?"
GIVE FEEDBACK ON FEEDBACK	"In recent feedback sessions, we focused mostly on the positive. More concrete, constructive feedback would ensure I do not have blind spots or stagnate in my growth."

The same is true for annual reviews: they are not an end to the cycle but the beginning of a new cycle. Remember: our goal is to support a *continuous* feedback culture. Once you receive your own annual review, set up time with your manager to turn any areas of development into a plan of attack, including timelines, development milestones, and a list of resources that can help. Managers, as part of this process, you should have action items to own as well. But all attorneys should approach their development with an ownership mindset.

CULTURE, NOT INFRASTRUCTURE

The tools in this chapter—combined with the prior investments in trust, ownership, and conflicts from earlier chapters—can help transform your feedback culture. These tools also highlight the fact that you do not need "HR infrastructure" to create a free exchange of feedback. For example, very few law firms have formal mechanisms to capture and relay peer feedback, let alone upward feedback, despite the ubiquity of these mechanisms—generally known as 360 feedback programs—in many other industries and companies. This is because some partners tend to be wary of these programs, making it a political hot potato.*

No matter. Such infrastructure is only a crutch. Nothing stops an attorney at any level from using the tools in this chapter to engage colleagues in candid feedback conversations directly. If your goal is to grow—and to help others grow—focus on *your* team and *your* relationships first. If you are successful in unlocking candid feedback, others will take notice.

Having a strong culture of continuous feedback is not just energizing—it's *liberating*. Knowing your colleagues are being honest with you will give you greater confidence to take risks

---

* To be clear, flipping a switch to allow anonymous feedback for partners after years without such a mechanism can be dangerous; it opens the floodgates to constructive but also unconstructive feedback, and the anonymity makes it impossible to follow up properly when feedback contains jarring stories or examples. Before doing so, I generally advise taking incremental steps—such as hosting a feedback training and considering a filtering process (known as moderated feedback)—to help prepare the culture for this change. Wherever possible, I prefer to focus on unlocking candid feedback (without anonymity) rather than rely so heavily on anonymous feedback channels.

and grow, trusting your team has your back. Once you experience that culture, you never want to work any other way.

Over the last few chapters, we covered the three essential ingredients for accountability:

1. Project management ensures all team members know what is expected. People cannot hold each other to high standards unless the expectations are clear.
2. Autonomy allows everyone the space they need to work and grow. This requires a balance: too much autonomy and the team will be overwhelmed; too little and the team's growth will be smothered by micromanagement.
3. Feedback provides the mechanism for learning from each other. Without a strong feedback culture, attorneys may have the desire to help each other grow, but they lack the means to do so.

Once teams combine these ingredients, the result is an unstoppable chain reaction of growth. In overly hierarchical law firms, a team leader must act as puppetmaster, pulling strings separately to direct each associate's individual workstream (and each associate's growth). This is incredibly inefficient. In teams with true accountability, the team members hold *each other* to high standards. They help *each other* grow. They sharpen *each other's* ideas. That is an exponential difference.

But going supersonic comes with a new set of challenges for managers and other senior leaders. When a plane is going that fast, a single rivet out of place can lead to catastrophic failure, which is why pilots are obsessive about inspecting their planes. The longer it takes to realize something is wrong, the greater the consequences. Similarly, leaders of high-performance teams must monitor their teams carefully so they can address and correct problems before they drag the team down. In the next chapter, we will discuss the tools leaders need to avoid blindspots.

CHAPTER 17

EVALUATING HIGH-PERFORMANCE LEGAL TEAMS

I n a strategic planning meeting a few years ago with a firm's leadership team, I asked the partners a simple question: "How do you identify your blind spots?"

One partner, clearly hesitant to answer, asked me to clarify what I meant by blind spots. I explained that while we would all love to be perfectly self-aware and have an equally perfect "pulse" on our team's needs and concerns, the reality is, we all have gaps in coverage. Sometimes we are unaware of our own weaknesses or missteps (personal blind spots), and other times we are unaware of pain points affecting our teams (organizational blind spots). So once again, I asked, "How do you identify your blind spots?"

Silence followed.

For context, the meeting was a precursor to an upcoming training series that I was delivering about building high-performance legal teams. Before these types of sessions, I like to meet with the senior members of the firm (or practice group) to align on training priorities. I want to know what they think about the current team dynamics, but I also have to keep in mind that leaders, even partners with a decade or more at the firm, often do not know the whole story. That is why I was asking about blind spots.

I broke the silence by drawing this simple diagram on a whiteboard:

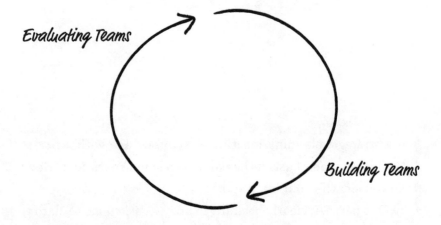

The diagram shows the "evaluate-build-repeat" loop. Many organizations want to *build* great teams, but they do not recognize their shortcomings in *evaluating* their teams. They want to jump in to talk about solutions but have not yet truly scoped out the problems in their organization.

Accountability requires a commitment to evaluation. Without that commitment, leaders who set out to build high-performance teams might not get far. After all, the initiatives they invest in will not always bear fruit. Efforts to build trust may backfire because team members believe leaders are disingenuous. An attorney's micromanagement may rob the team of opportunities to take ownership. The team might be consumed by a toxic conflict. Making matters more difficult, the problems leaders set out to solve can be a moving target. People come and go, cultures shift, and other forces constantly push teams out of equilibrium. At times, the work of improving a team can feel like "one step forward, two steps back."

Leaders must embrace this reality; there is no "set it and forget it" system. One must constantly evaluate progress and then use those findings to tailor the next set of team-building investments. That is how leaders can hold themselves accountable for delivering not just ideas but genuine impact. The evaluate-build-repeat cycle is something firms have to invest in properly, rather than just providing generic training sessions every few years. And much like a pilot going through a pre-flight checklist, a leader has to bring rigor and regularity to this evaluation process.

EARLIER INTEL IS BETTER INTEL

Too often, firms learn about their biggest organizational challenges only through exit interviews. Finally fed up, a senior associate resigns and unloads a heap of frustrations on the way out the door, only to leave practice group leaders frustrated that the associate never came to them to voice these concerns at a time when they could have done something useful. Worse yet, although the associate was not candid with the practice heads before departing, you can bet the associate had been freely complaining to peers the whole time. In other words, practice group leaders were not only out of the know; they were the *last* to know. Toxic narratives are now swirling, and leadership has to play catch-up.

How would this scene have unfolded differently if the firm had a way to surface issues before they festered into something toxic?

Leaders must hold themselves accountable for ensuring that systems are in place for evaluating and promptly surfacing the team's pain points. That toolkit includes self-awareness, assessments, pulse checks, one-on-ones, one-over-ones, and outside-in reviews—each of which we will discuss in more detail. The earlier we can surface issues with these tools, the easier it will be to make course corrections.

Team Health Assessments

Every time I start an engagement with a new organization (or a specific department or practice group within), I run a Team Health Assessment. This is a two-part exercise. First, I send all team members an anonymous survey with a set of quantitative and qualitative questions covering trust, ownership, conflict, and accountability. (You can find a sample survey in the Appendix.) That survey provides an overall sense of strengths and weaknesses so I know where to dig further. Then I conduct a series of interviews with a smaller sample of the team, going much deeper to surface specific examples and stories that help illuminate the underlying team dynamics. Once finished, I then compile a report for the senior leaders, anonymizing details to protect confidentiality, and we use that report to inform training priorities.

This two-part process is more informative than either surveys or interviews alone. Surveys provide useful information, but because they are usually anonymous, there is no way to follow up. It becomes too easy to dismiss some responses as outliers or ignore data points that seem ambiguous. Meanwhile, interviews provide greater depth but lack the breadth of surveys, since you cannot usually interview everyone, and even if you could, you cannot ask them every question under the sun in the limited time you have.

Although every team is different, consider using this one-two punch of surveys and interviews when you conduct an assessment of your team. The survey data provides a heat map and helps tailor the interview questions that follow, the combination of which is as efficient and informative as it gets.

It's important to note that you should not expect to score well in all aspects of this assessment. In fact, some of the results might make you cringe. These feelings are normal. An honest assessment is the only way forward. You have to establish a baseline, even if the baseline is rock bottom. But I promise: with time and commitment, any team can be turned around.

Pulse Checks

Team Health Assessments are a larger time investment, typically run once a year, and provide a comprehensive outlook on team dynamics. But in between those comprehensive assessments, "pulse checks" are shorter, more frequent surveys that can provide ongoing insight and direction with far less investment.

For example, the following three-question survey can be useful for practice groups wanting to track some key early indicators for attrition.

On a scale from 1 (strongly disagree) to 5 (strongly agree), rate these statements:
- I am delivering value to clients.

- My work-life balance is sustainable.
- I know what it takes to be successful in this role.

If someone is thinking of leaving the firm, there's a good chance one of these questions will trigger a negative response. After all, if one's work seems trivial, the hours are overwhelming, or there is no clear path to promotion, chances are that the attorney is poachable. To help decide what questions to include on these pulse check surveys, refer to the Team Health Assessment in the Appendix. Remember, your goal is to pick statements that relate to *your* biggest priorities for team health.

This survey is so simple that it can be run regularly with minimal burden on the team. After all, a three-question survey takes less than two minutes to complete. I recommend conducting these every two to four weeks so you can track team health closely.

But wait. Just three questions? And no space for free responses? And why repeat this survey over and over every few weeks?

The pulse check is not a holistic assessment tool; it is an early warning system. Think of it like a motion detector: by asking the same questions regularly, you get a clear quantitative baseline, and then when a score fluctuates materially up or down, the alarm sounds. At that point, you know to inquire further, either in team meetings or one-on-ones, about where the team is struggling and needs more support.

Imagine a deal team with a biweekly pulse check survey. Every other Monday, everyone receives an email reminder to take the survey and allots two minutes to complete it before starting their day. This is an easy habit to create. The scores seem stable for a few months. Then one day, there is a sudden shift; several scores drop a point or two. Something has happened, and you now have an opportunity to identify and address the issue in the moment, instead of waiting several months to uncover the problem in an annual assessment (or until after the attorney has left the firm altogether). If you had run the assessment every three to four months, you would rarely pick up on these pain points. Also, without more frequent data points, you will not know whether changes in scores are signs of genuine problems or just normal volatility, making the data you get back unreliable.

When a pulse check survey shows something amiss, your goal is to identify the specific issues or people who are, essentially, making a cry for help. But this has to be done delicately. If you do run these surveys anonymously, which is often more comfortable for teams, then you may want to follow up with the team to understand who is feeling the pain the most. To find that out, you have to proceed with empathy (see Chapter 11) and make clear that you want to provide support, not "out the instigator." If you mishandle this discussion, team members will likely provide artificially high scores in the future to avoid confrontation. But if you earn their trust, the pulse checks will uncover blind spots much sooner, when there is still time to do something useful.

Of all the tools for evaluating teams, lawyers are often the most skeptical of regular pulse checks. The idea of running surveys, even short ones, as often as every two weeks seems outlandish to many people. It may help to know that these kinds of tools are common in other industries. For example, many software engineering teams automate surveys like this in Slack, a popular chat platform, to keep the process simple.

For those who are unconvinced, think of it this way: if you are going to find the right tools for your team, you have to be willing to experiment with new ideas even if it means some of those ideas will miss the mark. That is part of the iteration process. Explain this to your team and enlist them in providing feedback so that you can improve your process over time.

If you are willing to experiment, you may find that pulse checks unlock new information you can use to catch problems early. Remember, in today's competitive market for talent, some firms will spend hundreds of thousands of dollars to replace a single associate. Anything you can do to avoid or delay an attorney's departure is time well spent.

One-On-Ones and One-Over-Ones

Earlier, in our discussion of one-on-ones, I mentioned how these meetings tend to devolve into purely tactical conversations, and how attorneys should leave space to ask more general questions that build trust.* But these are also opportunities to gather information about team (and individual) health. The trick is to *mean* it. Too often, such questions are posed as an afterthought, as though a meager "How's it going?" will trigger the attorney to unload all of their deepest concerns at your feet.

If you genuinely want to know how your team members are doing, you need to make that clear. For example, you might say, "I know we have had such tight turnarounds recently that we have not had a chance to connect beyond the tasks at hand. So let me take a step back and ask you, in all seriousness: how are you feeling? About the team, and the work? About the firm itself?"

Tone matters. Remember, your goal is to uncover impediments to trust, as well as other dysfunctions. You will only get this information if you make clear that you are there to help, not judge. You

---

* See Chapter 4, Exercise #1 ("Open-Ended Conversations").

can even think of these one-on-ones like an ongoing version of the interviews I referenced in the Team Health Assessment earlier.

But there is another type of one-on-one, called a "one-over-one" or "skip-level" one-on-one, which is an underutilized tool for shedding light on blind spots.

Even when I was a fairly junior team member, the senior partner on my case met with me at least once a quarter for a listening session. The senior partner would send questions in advance so I was not surprised, such as:

- How do you think the team is tracking (trajectory up or down)?
- What are the biggest roadblocks you are experiencing?
- What can your team leader be doing better? [The team leader was my supervisor, who in turn reported to the partner asking me this question.]
- What can I do better as the partner on this case?
- What else should I know/be asking?

These kinds of sessions are called "one-over-ones" or "skip levels" because they occur between a leader and the reports not one but two levels down from that leader. For example, at a law firm, a partner doing a skip-level session might meet with each junior associate who reports to the senior associate on the matter.

I highly recommend this framework for partners and other senior leaders. Do not rely solely on your direct reports to inform your evaluation. Speak directly to mid-level or junior associates on a regular basis, even if just for a brief check-in every two to three months, both to demonstrate that you care and to ensure that you have a complete picture.

Outside-In Reviews

The process of evaluating trust on a team can become overwhelming, not only because of the time it requires, but because none of these skills were taught in law school. You may also have to confront your own contributions to the team's fragility, which can place you in an awkward, even conflicting position.

Do not be afraid to bring outside parties in to help. Your HR team, professional development team, or external consultants can bring independence and objectivity to the process, not to mention an extra set of experienced hands. Although years of being on both sides of the process have made me cautious about using consultants (despite being one myself), it is hard to argue with the fact that extracting candid feedback is more difficult when the person doing it has power over the other person's future. You could try to acquire all information through anonymous surveys, but without the ability to follow up, these can feel like dead ends: you can read the comments, but you cannot ask for more examples, context, or clarifications.

———

Attorneys cannot just stop what they are doing and take several months to focus on team building. Instead, they have to build the plane while it's still in the air. Having the means to identify problems early can ensure that leaders spend their limited time and resources in the right places.

These systems are also the last piece of the accountability puzzle. Leaders need a way to hold *themselves* accountable for their teams' progress. Just as attorneys track billable hours, leverage ratios, expenses, and retention, they also need to track organizational health just as rigorously. The goal is not to blame; it is to help leaders set priorities. Without that accountability, any progress in building high-performance teams will be temporary.

By now, you can see why accountability is the final stage for building high-performance teams. We started with trust because that is what enables team members to stop focusing solely on self-preservation and start thinking about the needs of the team itself. That unlocks ownership, where team members embrace their role in helping the team achieve its goals, even if that means working to solve problems they did not themselves create. Once ownership takes hold, team members inevitably have different opinions about how best to proceed, sparking productive conflict that, if properly managed, drives sharper ideas and execution. Without these prerequisites, accountability—the willingness to hold each other to high standards—is not possible. Accountability is the culmination of our journey because it requires the cumulative effect of the other traits to thrive.

In software engineering, there is the notion of the "10x team," the kind of team that adds ten times as much value compared to other teams at the company. Although it sounds like hyperbole, it reflects a reality that exists when a combination of engineers comes together in perfect alignment to attack a challenge with unparalleled passion and commitment. Their success has nothing to do with their pedigrees, GPAs, or personality styles and everything to do with how they embody the key traits of high-performance teams.

That same level of teamwork, when unleashed in a law firm or other legal organization, can create an unstoppable force. If you want to build 10x legal teams, you know that there is no magical combination of resumes that will get you there. Great teams are more than just a combination of great individuals. They are not designed from a collection of spare parts; they are forged over time through intentional and collective leadership. If you are willing to put in the work, if you are patient and thoughtful, and if you embrace your role in improving the team, the 10x team could be yours.

CONCLUSION

For many attorneys, the legal work is their comfort zone. They would rather be consumed by case law, deal papers, policy memos, or other traditional billable tasks than have to navigate a tricky issue of team dynamics or dysfunction. As one senior associate put it, "I love my job. Except for all the 'people stuff.'"

I have heard this sentiment echoed by many attorneys across the profession. But we cannot compartmentalize the "people stuff" from the rest of "the job." Navigating team dynamics requires a constant commitment.

At the start of this book, I explained how this commitment must happen at three levels: the individual, the team, and the organization. Whoever you are, and whatever your title or tenure, I hope this book provides you with both the principles and, more importantly, the practical guidance you need to build a high-performance legal team.

But for those of you in a position to initiate broader changes at your organizations, you know how difficult it can be to lead this transformation at scale. Training sessions that purport to be action-oriented end up being little more than a flash in the pan. Committees form to own internal initiatives, but their ideas fail to gain traction. Why do our best efforts at organizational change often fall flat?

COURSE CORRECTIONS

As the saying goes, ideas are cheap; execution is everything. So too it is in legal organizations, especially law firms, where the same bad habits appear again and again when leaders attempt to drive organizational change. When I speak with professional development experts, many of them understand the limitations of existing approaches, but they are often no match for the hard-wired patterns and practices at law firms that hinder their transformation efforts.

Unless other leaders at the firm embrace certain changes, thereby creating a united front with those in professional development, they will continue to see the same lackluster results from their investments. I want to highlight three subtle but powerful course corrections in particular that, if adopted, will make these efforts far more impactful.

Correction #1: More Team Training, Not Management Training

We need a common language for teams, and that cannot happen if we always bifurcate our trainings between "managers" and "non-managers." This is especially common at law firms, where management training is frequently reserved for mid-level or senior associates. Partners are often excluded, as are junior associates.

Managers are also plucked for these trainings from across practice groups without regard for the unique pain points their teams face.

Proper team training requires a truly team-centric approach. This begins with dividing the organization into clusters based on practice groups or regional offices, or some combination of the two, consisting of no more than twenty or thirty attorneys who work together regularly and have their own subculture and challenges.* Then each training can be tailored to each team.

With this approach, the quality of training grows exponentially. Rather than generic advice, we can get in the weeds on what is holding *this* team back and design solutions that make sense *here*. The point of a training, after all, is to provoke action. In a generic "management" training, attorneys might walk away with a few ideas, but most will forget about those ideas the moment they return to their daily work. In a proper "team training," the entire group is present—including partners and associates—and the time is spent building *alignment* and *commitment* around specific action plans that address the top priorities of the team over the coming months.**

Professional development leaders may nod at this concept but bristle at the budget implications. Such skepticism is healthy. There are simply too many wasteful training programs that do little more than check a box and plant a few banal ideas. But if you start small

---

* You can theoretically divide these teams into smaller groups based on individual case teams or deal teams, but since those boundaries tend to be fluid, we do not need that level of granularity.

** There may still be a time and a place for traditional, cohort-based management training, such as when the organization needs to walk new managers through specific HR processes. But if the goal is to create stronger teams, the entire team should be involved.

with a pilot program in one practice group or office, you will see the ROI for yourself. And since the participants will include partners— the same people who make many of those budget decisions—they too will see that the value of this approach is far greater than traditional management trainings. A small pilot is usually enough to create a snowball effect as skeptics turn into evangelists.

Correction #2: Kickoffs, Not One-and-Done Programs

An outstanding team-centric training should be framed as a *kickoff*, not a one-and-done event. This kickoff might be formatted as a two-hour program, but everyone should understand that the real work comes *after* the session is over. This is because attorneys routinely underestimate the execution phase of organizational change. They may hear an idea, such as the recommendation of "retro" discussions to surface learnings after a major milestone, and they may be genuinely interested. But if that is where the discussion ends, the idea will end up on the backlog of already-overwhelmed partners and professional development managers to "handle implementation."

To land this point, start the implementation discussion *during* the kickoff program. For example, if attorneys are interested in making retros a regular part of their workflow, have them break into groups to brainstorm questions and potential implementation roadblocks. Not only is this early brainstorming informative for shaping the future proposal, but the act of thinking through execution, even for just a few minutes, can make the entire group more engaged in the idea. When people roll up their sleeves, they become more invested in the outcome. Then, when a smaller group takes over planning—hopefully a group comprised of more than just the usual players who support every organizational initiative—that group will have notes from these breakout sessions as a starting point to guide their discussion.

Since the goal of a kickoff program is to rouse the group to action, it is especially important to narrow down two or three concrete priorities for these sessions, rather than try to pack in a laundry list of best practices. If teams are focused on what they want to accomplish, they are much more likely to land on clear action items. That clarity is the key to building momentum.

Once the team achieves success on its initial set of priorities, they do not rest on their laurels. The process repeats, first with a team session to align on new goals and then with an implementation phase to execute whatever action plans the team agrees will propel them forward. Teams are always changing, with new challenges, new people, and new market pressures that require adaptation. Building teams requires an ongoing, collaborative process, not simply a flash-in-the-pan seminar.

Correction #3: "Agile," Not "Waterfall" (i.e., Planning for Iteration)

Most attorneys are terrified of making leadership mistakes, so much so that many would rather avoid trying something new than let their team members see them fail. That fear suffocates growth.

But this is not a fixed mindset. In other industries, the notion that one's initial idea will miss the mark is ingrained into the culture. Take the tech sector, for example. Imagine you have a "big idea" for a clever new app. You hire a team to plan out every feature your product will need, carefully estimate the time each component will take to design and code, and then build one component at a time. Once all of the components are ready, the product launches to customers, which is the first true test of the app. That process—known as the "waterfall" method—may sound reasonable, but it is entirely the *wrong* approach for most situations. If the product fails to win over customers, will you know why? Was it because it had too few features? Too many features? Was it too expensive? Something else? A massive, untested launch has too many variables at play, making it impossible to diagnose (and fix) whatever went wrong.

Instead, modern product developers have largely replaced the waterfall method with what is known as the "agile" method. In agile development, they test new ideas a little bit at a time—not all at once at the end—knowing this iterative process will help them isolate mistakes and correct them. Customers are consulted at every stage of development to provide concrete feedback. This guided evolution is crucial to growth.

For attorneys, a waterfall approach still makes sense for much of our *legal* work: we take in an assignment, review and research the issues carefully, and then deliver our advice (or other output) in a neat and tidy package. But we need a different strategy when thinking about internal or organizational changes. Leaders should not assign a new idea to a committee, have them spend months drafting a proposal, approve it, and then launch. When it fails—as it often does—there is no clear path forward, and it becomes yet another example of "something we tried a few years back" that didn't work. An agile approach would call for more testing and feedback along the way, with each step bringing the team closer to the right solution.

Leaders should embrace agile thinking for organizational development. They should also set expectations with the team, making clear that missteps *will* be part of the process. "We are going to try new things together, many of which will miss the mark," wrote one partner in an email introducing a series of initiatives around improved work-life balance. "We want your feedback to get things right." Reminders like this help set a positive (and collaborative) tone for the process of iteration to come.

THE RISE OF HYBRID TEAMS

Course corrections like these facilitate more impactful organizational development efforts, and these steps are especially important given the increasing popularity of hybrid and remote teams (generally known as "distributed teams").

Until the COVID-19 lockdowns that began in March 2020, many leaders did not realize how much of their culture and team success they owed to serendipitous interactions around the office. These were the "band-aids" that helped teams stay on track. Not sure how to tackle a new assignment? Tap a colleague on the shoulder. Miscommunication with a senior attorney? Clear it up when you see them later in the day. Trying to build career connections? A happy hour is around the corner.

Serendipity, of course, does not translate well to the hybrid or remote context. Some will see this as proof that the in-office experience is superior, but that thinking misses the point. While it is true that a distributed workforce can bring challenges, one does not necessarily cause the other. Remote and hybrid work simply *brings out an organization's lack of organization*. Serendipity can help ameliorate the impact of poor team alignment, unclear expectations, miscommunication, and lack of mentorship, but rather than rely on band-aids to cover up these problems, the solution here is to attack the underlying management gaps themselves.

That is where the principles of high-performance teams come into play. We do not have to rewrite the playbook; distributed teams still require trust, ownership, productive conflict, and accountability. But we need to be more intentional about every interaction to ensure that team members do not fall out of sync or feel isolated when working remotely—a common challenge. Such teams also need to invest more in documentation and project management to help them stay organized. And there are other nuances leaders should keep in mind, which I have written about in other contexts.* These nuances are important, but do not let them distract from the need to stay focused on the core principles of high-performance teams. If leaders are thoughtful about how they apply the principles in this book, attorneys can thrive in any environment, distributed or not.

ALL RISE

Despite some of the quips and jokes one hears about lawyers in pop culture, our profession still enjoys a special place in society. We are one of very few professions to enjoy self-governance, for example. We write our own code of ethics and decide for ourselves who can enter and remain within our ranks. And when the judge enters the courtroom, we ask everyone, not just the lawyers, to rise out of respect for the proceedings. You will not see that behavior in the worlds of marketing, software engineering, or finance.

Although our profession has evolved, many still hold the law—and lawyers—on a pedestal. But that reputation suffers, both

---

* For more on tactics for managing remote and hybrid legal teams, visit *allrisebook.com/hybrid-teams*.

inside and outside the profession, when lawyers pursue results at the expense of their colleagues and their teams. Too many lawyers become jaded by the lack of leadership they see in their organizations, or worse yet, some believe that one cannot manage teams with compassion but still be competitive. I hope that this book shows a better way, a path that allows for leadership and development without sacrificing determination.

Do not be daunted by the work ahead. Many organizations turn themselves around without the benefit of large training budgets or outside consultants; they simply have the commitment to put in the work and the willingness to learn from their mistakes along the way. In the Appendix, you will find a roadmap you can use to get started, and you can find many of the tools, templates, and frameworks described in this book at allrisebook.com.

Those who internalize the principles of high-performance teams will have a major advantage in their careers. They will be the kind of leaders others want to follow, the ones who have influence far beyond their clients, cases, or deals. And as they invest the time in showing others how to lead, they have an incredible, multiplicative effect: those they train will go on to build their own teams, creating a chain reaction that spreads through an organization—and beyond. As they rise, the entire profession rises with them.

TEAM BUILDING PROGRAM TEMPLATE

The template below is included as a starting point to help leaders who desire deeper, transformational change on their teams. It is similar to the program I use with law firms through my own consulting and training company. But even if you do not have the budget to bring in external resources, you can still be successful by leveraging internal experts and thought leaders. This template and other resources are available at *allrisebook.com*.

Step 1: Diagnose

 A. Conduct the Team Health Assessment (survey + interviews)
   i. A survey template can be found in Appendix B. The survey should be distributed to all team members, including team leaders (e.g., partners). The goal is to develop a heat map of strengths and weaknesses for further inquiry.

ii. Conduct confidential interviews with a representative sample of team members (including team leaders), asking for specific examples related to the strengths and weaknesses surfaced in the survey. An outsider, such as someone from the HR or professional development team, may be necessary to encourage candor. The goal is to resolve ambiguities from the survey and extract specific examples to enrich the assessment.

iii. Compile key themes into a report for the leadership team.

B. Meet with the leadership team to review the Team Health Assessment and set training priorities.

Step 2: Introduce the Principles of High-Performance Teams

A. Format: Full-day and half-day training sessions will be the most impactful. A two-hour training can also work but will require significant adaptation of the agenda suggested below. Be sure to include all members of the team (e.g., both partners and associates).

B. Description: Frame this training session as a kickoff, not a one-and-done event. The goals are (i) to build a common vocabulary around the principles and processes we need to be successful; (ii) to open a dialogue about where we are and the distance to travel; and (iii) to commit to the role we *all* play in the team's improvement.

C. Sample Agenda:
   i. Begin with an overview of key traits of high-performance teams: trust, ownership, productive conflict, and accountability.
   ii. Open an honest dialogue by dividing participants into breakout groups (four to six people) and prompting them to share their personal opinions on which of the "agree or disagree" statements in the survey (see Appendix B) illustrate the team's current strengths and weaknesses.
   iii. Dive deeper into each of the key traits on high-performance teams. (In a two-hour program, select at most two to three traits for deep dives.) For each trait, in addition to brief lectures where necessary, use breakout sessions to encourage concrete, actionable discussions. For example, use the Motivation Sharing Exercise and Social Styles assessments to build trust (see Chapter 4).
   iv. If leaders have specific proposals in mind to address pressing concerns, have the team discuss those proposals in breakout groups to encourage ownership and sharpen the implementation plan. Collect any feedback from these breakouts for later.
   v. End the session with a review of action items. If more time is required to consider proposals, be clear about who is in charge of each effort and the expected deadline.

Step 3: Monitor Progress

A. After the introductory training session, set a timeline to follow up on any agreed-upon action items.

B. Every three to six months, conduct an abbreviated survey (see "Pulse Check Surveys" in Chapter 17) to check in on the biggest areas of concern from the Team Health Assessment.

C. Conduct additional training sessions every six months based on the specific needs of the group (e.g., Feedback or Delegation). For example, each chapter of this book reflects one (or more than one) training session from my own curriculum.

D. Every twelve months, repeat the full Team Health Assessment (both the survey and interviews) to set new training priorities.

Step 4: Rinse and Repeat

A. Typically, after three to four years, teams will need to restart the cycle, beginning with a refresher on the core principles of trust, ownership, productive conflict, and accountability. (This also ensures that new employees do not miss these fundamental concepts, though they can also be trained via "catch-up" sessions.)

B. Before restarting the cycle, gather feedback on the training program as a whole, iterating as needed to ensure the program meets the needs of your particular organization.

TEAM HEALTH ASSESSMENT: SURVEY TEMPLATE

A survey like this can be run for any legal organization, but to demonstrate precise language, this particular example is written for a single practice group of a large firm. If the intention is to run this survey across multiple practice groups, departments, or divisions, include the question at the end that asks participants to specify which group they serve so that the results can be separated by team. You can download this template at *allrisebook.com*.

Remember that a thorough Team Health Assessment consists of not just this survey but interviews as well. Use the results of this survey to inform those interview questions.

Survey Questions

1. Please review the following statements and indicate how well you agree with each on a scale from 1 ("strongly disagree") to 10 ("strongly agree")*:

   1.1. [*Trust*] Team members readily admit to each other when they have made a mistake.

   1.2. [*Trust*] Team members are open about their strengths and weaknesses.

   1.3. [*Ownership*] Team members identify problems and solve them on their own without being asked.

   1.4. [*Ownership*] Team members put the needs of the team ahead of their own personal interests.

   1.5. [*Ownership*] I feel engaged and interested in the work that I do.

   1.6. [*Ownership*] I understand and appreciate the group's priorities and strategic direction.

   1.7. [*Productive Conflicts*] Team members readily voice their concerns.

   1.8. [*Productive Conflicts*] Managers are aware of and help resolve conflicts on the team productively.

   1.9. [*Accountability*] I know what it takes to be successful in my role.

   1.10. [*Accountability*] I regularly receive actionable, constructive feedback.

---

* The [bracketed headers] are informative only and can be removed prior to sending the survey. They are intended as a reference for organizing the data after collection.

1.11. [*Accountability*] I regularly provide upward feedback.

1.12. [*Accountability*] Team members are trusted to get the job done with minimal supervision or micromanagement.

1.13. [*Equity & Inclusion*] I feel my unique background and identity are valued.

1.14. [*Equity & Inclusion*] All team members have equal opportunities to advance.

1.15. [*Equity & Inclusion*] I have someone at the firm who actively supports me in my career (whether or not the person is a formal mentor).

1.16. [*Equity & Inclusion*] Practice group leaders care about what I think.

1.17. [*Other*] My pace of work is sustainable.

1.18. [*Other*] My compensation is reasonable given my role and contributions.

2. The leadership team is on the _____ track regarding our culture.

    ☐ Right   ☐ Wrong

3. Aside from compensation, what factors do you value most as you continue your career at this organization? (Select at most 2 options.)

    ☐ More responsibility
    ☐ More creativity
    ☐ Clearer advancement opportunities
    ☐ Better management
    ☐ Better work-life balance
    ☐ Better team culture
    ☐ Other (Please specify) _____

4. My job performance would be most improved by: (Select at most 2 options.)

    ☐ More formal training
    ☐ More clearly defining metrics for my performance
    ☐ More efficient meetings
    ☐ Making compensation and promotional opportunities more transparent
    ☐ Providing clear constructive feedback
    ☐ Providing better mentorship opportunities
    ☐ Colleagues or managers improving their management skills
    ☐ Increasing social activities
    ☐ Reducing the pace or amount of work
    ☐ None of these
    ☐ Other (Please specify) _____

5. As a place to work, what are the practice group's greatest strengths?

_____

_____

6. As a place to work, what are the practice group's most significant weaknesses?

_____

_____

7. Is there anything else you would like to add?

_____

_____

8. Please indicate your level:
   - ☐ Associate <= 4 years
   - ☐ Associate 5+ years
   - ☐ Partner/Counsel

9. How long have you worked at this firm?
   - ☐ < 12 months
   - ☐ 1-4 years
   - ☐ > 4 years

10. I work in the _____ practice group.
    - ☐ [Insert appropriate options]

Additional Considerations

When replicating this assessment process with your team, there are a few "watch outs" to keep in mind.

1. **Survey design is a discipline unto itself**. I oversaw the user research team at a tech company for many years, a team with experts who could spot costly survey mistakes a mile away. If you do not have rich experience with survey design, be humble and ask for help. Your organization may have internal experts. If not, hire someone or just stick to templates that have already been well-tested (like the one above).

2. **Less is more.** When writing your own questions, be cognizant that adding questions will decrease both the response rate and the quality of responses. (This is known as "survey fatigue.") If you pair the survey with interviews, as I recommend, you only need the survey to *inform* the interviews, not replace them.

3. **"Everyone" means *everyone*.** This can also be a great opportunity to include nonlawyers, such as paralegals, assistants, IT, and others who are just as integral to the team's success. Also, do not not leave partners or other leaders out of the Team Health Assessment. When I work with law firms, I include partners in both my surveys and my sample interviews. In fact, unhealthy dynamics among leaders are often the most important to uncover, since they trickle down into every aspect of the team.

4. **"Team" means *team*.** The Team Health Assessment is most useful when employed at a team level, as opposed to trying to run a single, giant assessment against an entire organization. After all, we are trying to understand how a team functions, and every team may have its own subculture. For example, at large law firms, I typically run the assessment for each practice group separately, and for groups larger than fifty, I typically break it down further, such as by office or region.*

---

* Practically speaking, the survey itself can be deployed across multiple groups at once as long as you ask questions that help you segment the data, but there is no similar shortcut for the interview process. For example, if I isolate a...

5. **Candor is currency.** Honesty tends to be the hard part. While surveys can be anonymized, interviews cannot. For very healthy cultures, a team leader can conduct the interviews personally and still achieve candor. Sometimes, it is better to use an "inside-outsider," like an HR representative or a leader from another group. Other times, only a true outsider like a consultant can earn sufficient trust to bring forth honest answers. The best approach will vary from team to team.

...subset of thirty to forty attorneys, such as by practice group and region, I would typically conduct five to ten interviews within that group.

NOTES

1   Patrick M. Lencioni, *The Five Dysfunctions of a Team: A Leadership Fable* (San Francisco: Jossey-Bass, 2002).

2   Thomson Reuters Institute and Georgetown University Law Center on Ethics and the Legal Profession, *2022 Report on the State of the Legal Market: A Challenging Road to Recovery*, 2022, 8, https://www.thomsonreuters.com/en-us/posts/wp-content/uploads/sites/20/2022/01/State-of-Legal-Market-Report_Final.pdf.

3   Vivia Chen, "Big Law's Great Resignation: Why I Don't Believe the Hype," Bloomberg Law, November 12, 2021, https://news.bloomberglaw.com/business-and-practice/big-laws-great-resignation-why-i-dont-believe-the-hype.

4   Mark J. Masson and Katie Styler, "Forum: The Attrition Antidote— Anticipating (and Preempting) Attrition through People Intelligence," Thomson Reuters, June 21, 2022, https://www.thomsonreuters.com/en-us/posts/legal/forum-spring-2022-attrition-antidote/.

5   Thomson Reuters Institute, *2022 Report on the State*, 20–21.

6   Charles Duhigg, "What Google Learned From Its Quest to Build the Perfect Team," *New York Times Magazine*, February 25, 2016, https://www.nytimes.com/2016/02/28/magazine/what-google-learned-from-its-quest-to-build-the-perfect-team.html.

7   For a longer list of privileges to consider, see Karen Caltin, *Better Allies: Everyday Actions to Create Inclusive, Engaging Workplaces*, 2nd ed., (Better Allies Press, 2021), 22-27.

8   Deborah Tannen, *You Just Don't Understand: Women and Men in Conversation* (New York: William Morrow Paperbacks, 2007), 77.

9   Ijeoma Oluo, *So You Want to Talk about Race*, (New York: Seal Press, 2018).

10   Jennifer Brown, *Inclusion: Diversity, the New Workplace & the Will To Change*, (Connecticut: Purpose Driven Publishing, 2016).

11   Gerardo Alcazar, "Diverse and Inclusive Teams: They Simply Work Better Together," American Bar Association, published August 3, 2021, https://www.americanbar.org/groups/litigation/committees/woman-advocate/articles/2021/summer2021-diverse-and-inclusive-teams-they-simply-work-better-together/.

12   Stanley McChrystal, *Team of Teams: New Rules of Engagement for a Complex World* (New York: Penguin Books Limited, 2015), 225–29.

13   Jerald Greenberg, "Promote Procedural and Interactional Justice to Enhance Individual and Organizational Outcomes," in *Handbook of Principles of Organizational Behavior: Indispensable Knowledge for Evidence-Based Management*, ed. Edwin Locke (Hoboken, N.J: Wiley, 2012), 255. https://doi.org/10.1002/9781119206422.ch14.

14   Cecilia M. Falbe and Gary Yukl, "Consequences for Managers of Using Single Influence Tactics and Combinations of Tactics," *Academy of Management Journal* 35, no. 3 (1992): 638–52. https://doi.org/10.5465/256490.

15   Kenneth W. Thomas and Ralph H. Kilmann, "The Social Desirability Variable in Organizational Research: An Alternative Explanation for Reported Findings," *Academy of Management Journal* 18, no. 4 (1975): 745, https://doi.org/10.5465/255376.

16   Ralph H. Kilmann, "A Brief History of the Thomas-Kilmann Conflict Mode Instrument (TKI)," Kilmann Diagnostics, accessed August 26, 2022, https://kilmanndiagnostics.com/a-brief-history-of-the-thomas-kilmann-conflict-mode-instrument/.

17   Kilmann, "Brief History of the TKI."

18   Chris Voss, *Never Split the Difference: Negotiating As If Your Life Depended On It* (New York: HarperCollins Publishers, 2016), 112–16.

19   Linda Babcock and Sara Laschever, *Women Don't Ask: The High Cost of Avoiding Negotiation—and Positive Strategies for Change* (New York: Bantam, 2007), 93–122.

20   Deborah Small et al., "Who Goes to the Bargaining Table? The Influence of Gender and Framing on the Initiation of Negotiation," *Journal of Personality and Social Psychology* 93, no. 4 (2007): 600–13, http://doi.org/10.1037/0022-3514.93.4.600.

21   Roger Fisher, William L. Ury, and Bruce Patton, *Getting to Yes: Negotiating Agreement Without Giving In*, 3rd ed. (Boston: Houghton Mifflin, 2011), 8–15.

22   Fisher et al., *Getting to Yes.*

23   William Ury, *Getting Past No: Negotiating in Difficult Situations* (New York: Bantam, 1991).

24 Voss, *Never Split the Difference.*

25 Chuck Yeager and Leo Janos, *Yeager: An Autobiography* (New York: Bantam, 1985), 138–66.

26 Yeager and Janos, *Yeager,* 164–65.

27 Jason Fried and David Heinemeier Hansson, *Remote: Office Not Required* (New York: Currency, 2013), 185.

28 Gino Wickman, *Traction: Get a Grip on Your Business* (Dallas: BenBella Books, 2012), 139.

29 American Bar Association, Model Rules of Professional Conduct Rule 1.1 (2022).

30 American Bar Association, Model Rules of Professional Conduct Rule 5.1 (2022).

31 David Marquet, *Turn the Ship Around!: A True Story of Turning Followers into Leaders* (New York: Random House, 2012), 92.

32 Sharon K. Parker, Caroline Knight, and Anita Keller, "Remote Managers Are Having Trust Issues," *Harvard Business Review,* July 30, 2020, https://hbr.org/2020/07/remote-managers-are-having-trust-issues.

ACKNOWLEDGMENTS

I am grateful to the many, many people who contributed both directly and indirectly to *All Rise*. First and foremost, there are the outstanding attorneys who took time they certainly did not have to provide feedback and ideas during development, especially Aisha Greene, Lauren Hakala, Mikeisha Anderson Jones, Tara Mikkilineni, J.D. Moss, and David Wolfson. I will never forget their generosity. My deepest thanks as well to the diligence of Emilie Jimenez, Emily Johnson (who designed the cover), Eliece Pool, John van der Woude, and others who helped bring this project to print.

In writing a book about teams, I could not help but reflect on the wonderful colleagues, leaders, and educators who helped shape my own management philosophy. First and foremost, I want to thank my all-time favorite bosses, not only for their support in my career, but for their positive examples of leadership, many of which appear directly in the pages of this book. These include Aftab Hussain, Robert Keeling, and TJ Leonard.

Next, I want to thank the Storyblocks family for their patience, enthusiasm, and feedback over many years as I attempted to develop my management style, especially Sydney Carlton (who also gave comments on the book itself), Jordan Chasnoff, Jason Chong, Jonathan Fulton, Nikki Heidelberg, Joel Holland, Kristin Keohan, Rashmi Ripley, Srey Sankar, Ashley Sansing, Michael Sherman, and Ben Wolfram.

And while we're on the subject of incredible teams that changed my life, I have to mention Team "972" and the family that formed around it, especially Mostafa Abdelkarim, Samantha Bateman, David Cross, Toby Heytens, Rakesh Kilaru, Jamar Walker, and Daniel Young, all of whom are world-class attorneys and role models for the profession.

Many colleagues from my early days at Sidley Austin continue to support my teaching, whether serving as guest speakers in my law school classes, co-presenting at conferences, or simply debating legal ethics late into the night, including Nicholas Alexiou, Sara Beardsley, Chanda Betourney, and Cara Viglucci Lopez, among others mentioned already.

I want to thank my students and colleagues at the University of Virginia School of Law for the joy they bring to my teaching. I am particularly lucky to have the support and partnership of Molly Shadel, an incomparable professor, author, and presenter. Nor would I be where I am today without the mentorship of professors Kenneth Elzinga, Karen Moran, and Larry Sabato.

If this book contains even one split infinitive, I hope the Honorable T.S. Ellis, III, views it as an homage to our time together in his chambers, where he taught me and my extraordinary co-clerk, Tyler McGaughey, to embrace a deeper commitment to the craft of legal writing, and for sharing with us his wisdom, warmth, and experience.

Finally, to my wife, Emily, I am sorry you effectively had to read this book three times, but it is because of you that each version was better than the last. You are the greatest teammate of them all.

ABOUT THE AUTHOR

Ben Sachs is an expert in management, strategy, and negotiation. He serves on the teaching faculty of the University of Virginia School of Law and has trained thousands of attorneys around the world through CLEs, seminars, and workshops. Ben also provides direct consulting and training services for government and private sector organizations in the United States and internationally. His past clients cover a wide range of industries, including law firms, tech companies, media, retail, and more.

Ben's professional career spans law and business, first serving as a litigator at Sidley Austin LLP and then as a strategic management consultant at Boston Consulting Group before moving to Storyblocks, a technology and stock media company repeatedly named among the fastest-growing companies by Inc. magazine. At Storyblocks, Ben served as General Counsel and Chief Operating Officer, overseeing product development, marketing, analytics, content acquisition, and strategy, ultimately helping secure the company's private-equity acquisition in 2020.

Ben earned his B.A. as an Echols Scholar and Jefferson Scholar at the University of Virginia and his J.D. from the University of

Virginia School of Law, where he graduated Order of the Coif and a member of the Virginia Law Review. After law school, he served as a law clerk for Judge T.S. Ellis, III, in the United States District Court for the Eastern District of Virginia in Alexandria. He lives outside Washington, D.C., with his wife and two children.

Printed in the USA
CPSIA information can be obtained
at www.ICGtesting.com
CBHW020753230324
5660CB00001B/2